Fiddyment/Crawford

Daniel Fiddyment (1770-1855) & Sarah Wells (1780-1860) m. 1807 England
_____

John (1809-1874)	William (1814-1878)
m.1837 Sophia Boggs (1813-1888)	m. 1836 Hannah Knivet (1815-19

Walter J. 1837-1905

Daniel 1837-1906

Frederick 1839-1903

Hannah 1842-1925

Walter J. 1845-1900

Mary A. 1848-1850

|

Walter (1826-1851)

m. 1850 Elizabeth Jane Crawford (1830-1906)

|

Walter 1850-1933

G. W. Crawford (1800-1880) & Mary Geddes (1801-   ) m. ~1823 Ireland

Mary (1824-1896)	Marjorey (1826-1891)
m. 1840 Armstead Runyon (1800-1876)	m.1846 C.V. Talmadge (1822-1914)
Oliver 1846-1846	Emma Caroline 1846-1897
Victoria 1847-	Samuel 1850-1932
Henry 1849-	Harriet 1852-1932
Albert 1854-	Mary Jane 1853-1939
William 1856-1940	Henrietta 1857-1938
Charles E. 1857-1944	Clara A. 1857-1864
Frederick 1860-	Charles L. 1862-1886
Emma 1875-	Josephine 1862-1900
	Anna M. 1869-1947

|

Elizabeth Jane

850 Walter Fiddyment (1826-1851)   m. 1855 George Hill (1829-1861)   m. 1868 A. Atkinson (1826-1903)

| | [no children]

Walter 1850-1933   Martha 1855-1930

James 1856-1864

John 1856-1926

Frank 1858-1882

Georgia 1861-1916

Walk With Me, I Want To Tell You Something

The Story of the Roseville Fiddyment Family

by

Christina Richter with David Fiddyment

Library of Congress Control Number: 2013951572

ISBN-13: 978-0-9891360-9-9
Walk With Me, I Want To Tell You Something, Softcover Edition 2013

ISBN-13: 978-0-9910132-1-0
Walk With Me, I Want To Tell You Something, Hardcover Edition 2013
Printed in the United States of America

For more information about special discounts for bulk purchases, please contact 3L Publishing at 916.300.8012 or log onto our website at www.3LPublishing.com.

Book design by Erin Pace-Molina
Cover art by Evangeline Johnson

This book is dedicated to Elizabeth Jane Crawford Fiddyment Hill Atkinson.
Ultimately it was she who was the inspiration behind this project.
Without her this remarkable family history would not have been possible.

Acknowledgements

Putting a book like this together requires support from many people.

First and foremost the Fiddyment family, especially David and Dolly, who made the dream of this book turn into reality. Each time Dolly located more family letters I was thrilled, and each interview with David left me with feelings of grand nostalgia. It was my honor to write their family's story.

My own family, husband Mark, daughters Audrey and Anna, and my father Bob, started hearing about this project back in 2005. They listened, for years, as I regaled them with discoveries about the Fiddyment family and their relation to the Donner Party, the California Gold Rush, the railroad, and the little town once called Junction. They shared in my excitement as they discovered, with me, how Roseville came to be the wonderful city it is today.

The day I met the curator of the Roseville Carnegie Museum, Phoebe Astill, was the day light truly shined on my project. Phoebe has been by my side giving me history lessons, reassurance, and a little ribbing now and then to keep me in line.

There are certain members of the Fiddyment family who were not only great resources for me, but grew to become some of my dearest friends. Eric Fiddyment always had positive answers when I bombarded him with questions. Denise Fiddyment was my most enthusiastic cheerleader and supporter. Erica Fiddyment Matney was truly a blessing as she lent her talent just when the project started to overwhelm me.

Finally, I am especially appreciative of my dear friend Lori Hurst Richardson. In the eleventh hour of crunch time, she put her life on hold to read my final chapters. She gave me her edits, insight and unending support.

I am also hugely grateful to all of the historians, archivists, curators, writers and other experts who gave generously of their time and provided research or advice.

Thank you! All of you! It has been a wonderful journey! ❧

Contents

Preface

A Walk with David Fiddyment

The man of 20 is quite different from the man of 50, and at 90 he's by far more different than at any other time in his life. As the pages of time turn, people change and so do communities. Time tends to erase old landmarks, neighborhoods, and even entire sections of a place.

One day I had the privilege of taking a walk with David on his old ranch property in west Roseville. The stately homestead brought a smile to his face and his descriptions of the past were animated. He recalled where the dirt roadways on the ranch used to be, and where the buildings that once housed the lifeblood of the Fiddyment family used to stand. As we approached the proud, old home he quickly told me everything as though he might suddenly forget.

"The well was right here, and the garden was just beyond that fence," he said as clear as if it were yesterday. Then he went on to describe the cooling shed and the smoke house, speaking with pride and a hint of longing for those younger days on the ranch. He made sure that I understood that both of these old

brick buildings had been an integral part of Fiddyment life on the ranch. "Grandpa's father-in-law was a very talented brick mason, and he did a lot to contribute to the ranch's success," he explained as we inspected the time-worn walls.

The two structures had long ago been abandoned of their original purpose, but a barn owl had taken residence at the top of the smokehouse, pleasing us that the old structure was still being put to good use.

Looking past the immediate house and buildings, David pointed to and described the places where a barn, turkey house and blacksmith shop once stood. Then he spotted an object of peculiar interest a ways off in the field; it looked to be a very large copper pot, and he wanted to walk the distance to see if he could figure out what it was.

Leaning on me, he stepped with a slow but steady pace and all the while he was explaining things, like how particular types of grass that grew in the fields were good for cattle and sheep grazing, where the ranch hands did most of their work, and how the family made their provisions last through the winter. He slowed a bit here and there but insisted we keep on moving.

We reached the gigantic copper pot and while he could identify the turkey-cooling bin and a few other items close by, he wasn't able to recall just what that large pot was ever used for. Puzzled and looking a little defeated, he brightened when he spotted a small group of oak trees a little further in the distance. He said he wanted to walk among them.

As we approached the shade of the old oaks, he gave me details about how he and the other kids would come and play in this space. When he was growing up it was far enough away from the house he explained, to be the secret area for he and his playmates. Pointing to a small stream, he told me how his dad had diverted the creek so that the house and other buildings would be in less danger of flooding.

As we walked into the coolness under the canopy of the sprawling branches, his pace quickened and he headed straight toward one of the big oaks as if it were his long-lost friend. "This," he said pointing out specific trees, "was where we kids used to sit. My dad put a board in the fork of each of these trees and we would use them as benches." Then he reminisced about younger carefree days when he and his friends and cousins would sit under the tree canopy and talk and play for hours.

This group of old oaks was a special place, and it was good to be with him as he recalled his memories and smiled. His face was a reflection of a man longing once again for his youth and at the same time, loving the joys he had experienced throughout his life.

That day I vowed to take it all in with him. ❧

Prologue

The following pages are the story of the Roseville, California Fiddyment family. It starts with their earliest ancestor and her arrival in California in the early 1850's. Elizabeth Jane Crawford Fiddyment came to Northern California a widow with a baby boy. She came to this area not as a gold miner, but as a young woman who wanted to start a new life in the promising land of California. Her story alone is one of incredible perseverance against the odds. The story continues with her son, Walter, his son, Russell, and finally, David.

The boys are the stock of the original California pioneer. The entire story is one of struggles and triumph, and is a historical glimpse into life as it once was here in Placer County, and the area once dubbed "Junction" that eventually grew up to become the city of Roseville.

The book ends with chapters about David's life. How his family's roots influenced him, and how he, the last generation of farmers, made the transition from the old generations to the new.

David Fiddyment and I have been working on this book for a very long time. For a year or so he and I spent nearly every Friday together talking about his family and the generations of Fiddyments that have lived out on the ranch. During our times together I discovered other things too: pictures, letters — some over a hundred years old, newspaper clippings and priceless relics. I've endeavored to put it all together, here, to tell the story of this venerable old family.

What is their story? It is not new, nor is it radical. In fact, it is as old as humankind itself. It is actually about humanity. Those whom we love and who take care of us, who nourish our children, and work our ranch. Those who call us mom and dad, and sister and brother, and uncle and aunt. It is about people who see each other for who they are and still love as a family through it all.

Marcus Cicero, a Roman statesman and philosopher, once said, "To be ignorant of what occurred before you were born is to remain always a child. For what is the worth of human life, unless it is woven into the life of our ancestors by the records of history?"

It is with this sentiment that David and I bring to you the story of the Roseville Fiddyment family. ❧

1

Before California

Nothing could have prepared the young mother for the shock of what was about to happen. Nothing in her Irish upbringing, her family's immigration struggles, or her girl's seminary schooling could offer her any solace. It was a heart-breaking tragedy — and she had no choice but to face it.

On Thursday, April 10, 1851, the bustling town of Joliet, Illinois was overcast and chilly. [Elizabeth] Jane Crawford Fiddyment was hastily bundling up her baby for an outing. Her husband Walter was at work and she wanted to take in some spring air before the rain set in. Walter Jr. was a beautiful, strapping five-month-old boy and easily the pride and joy of both their families. Jane and her husband had been married for just 14 months, but they lived in a small town and the Crawfords and the Fiddyments knew each other well.

Jane's husband, Walter, had been the youngest of the Fiddyment brothers to immigrate to America from England. In 1843 he sailed from his homeland as an eager young man of 18. After six long months of traveling, Walter made it to Lockport, Illinois and joined his brother John and his family. America was the Promise Land and altogether the Fiddyment brothers were doing quite well.

Walter easily settled into American life and successfully gained employment at the same distillery where his brother once worked. The brothers were from a family of English distillers and young America willingly rewarded their talents. The 18-year-old lad grew to be a successful, handsome man and in 1850 he attracted the eye of a young Irish girl by the name of Jane Crawford. The two were married and a baby boy was born to the couple a year later. By 1851 Walter's employer had advanced him to supervisor, and he and Jane anticipated a promising future for their family in the rapidly growing area.

But it was a time of great change in America. In the early 1850's people were reading rousing newspaper articles about the California Gold Rush and dreaming of a journey west and getting rich. The Industrial Revolution was in full swing and from the east coast cities to the Midwest farmlands, many people were changing their lifestyles. New modes of transportation

English born Walter Fiddyment immigrated to the United States in 1826 at age 17. He was attacked at his workplace in Joliet, Illinois on April 9, 1851 and died from his wounds the next day. He left behind a nine-month-old baby boy and his wife Elizabeth Jane.

such as canal boats, steam ships, and the massive locomotive were preferred over the rugged journeys of horse and buggy. In the cities especially, machines and factory-based work were becoming the norm for employment. Most of these transitions were welcome changes, but unfortunately some were very difficult.

Labor laws were basically nonexistent and workers were sorely mistreated. Long hours, poor conditions, and very little pay caused struggles and conflict. In the early 1850's labor anxiety ran high with over-worked employees and menacing, even disastrous encounters sometimes occurring. The vast unrest of the time could have easily been at the heart of the shocking tragedy.

Earlier that particular day in 1851, angry shouts were heard coming from the Joliet Woodruff distillery where Walter Fiddyment was supervisor. Harsh words were being exchanged between Fiddyment and a man named Thomas Bwyn. A ghastly skirmish ensued.

A little while later, Jane was set to take her walk when several men, carrying her husband, came rushing toward her. The rain had begun to fall. Walter was unconscious and was bleeding from several very serious stab wounds. Jane showed the men to a bedroom where her husband's wounded body was carefully laid down, while a physician took over his care.

Word of the event traveled quickly. Family members rushed to her side as Jane cared for her husband in his last hours of life. It was a day before Walter succumbed to his wounds. He died on April 11, 1851.

Jane wrapped her arms tightly around her baby boy as she stood in the open doorway of their home. Through stinging tears she gazed upon the last bits of melting snow on that cold day and choked back her hopes for a future she could no longer have. The clouds reflected the dark hour as she came to the full realization that now she would have to face her life as a widowed, single mother.

But she couldn't think about that now. Change was upon her and there was enormous responsibility at hand. She took a deep breath and summoned the strength and courage to go on.

Born into an Irish immigrant family, Elizabeth Jane Crawford married Walter Fiddyment in Joliet, Illinois in February 1850.

The *Joliet Signal Newspaper* of the day reports Walter Fiddyment's murder account as follows:

"An altercation, about some trivial matter, took place between Mr. Feddyment and a man named Thomas Bwyn, in one of the rooms of the distillery. The latter, using insulting language, was ordered out of doors by the former and on refusing to go, after some further quarrel, Mr. Feddyment put him out at the door. Bwyn returned again and Feddyment took hold of him the second time to put him out, when he stabbed Feddyment with a knife, in three different places in his abdomen, letting his intestines out; besides giving him several cuts on his arms and in his side. Feddyment, by the assistance of a man who was present, became disengaged and fled, but being pursued by Bwyn, notwithstanding his wounds, seized hold of a shovel, turned and dealt his pursuer such a blow as to fell him to the floor. After which Feddyment escaped into an adjoining room and fastened the door against his assailant. Upon the arrival of the Physician and others at the scene, the victim was found lying on the floor in a state of insensibility. He was carried to his residence — his wounds were examined and pronounced mortal, and he lingered in the most excruciating agony until the following day, when he breathed his last.

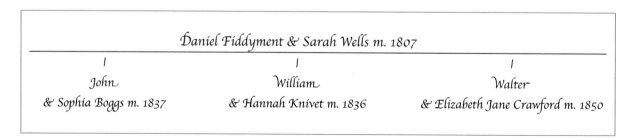

Daniel Fiddyment & Sarah Wells m. 1807

John	William	Walter
& Sophia Boggs m. 1837	& Hannah Knivet m. 1836	& Elizabeth Jane Crawford m. 1850

FORM 2080   8-29-24

No. ____250____

PROBATE COURT

WILL COUNTY, ILL.

In the Matter of the Estate of

WALTER FIDDYMENT

DECEASED

55

Box No. ____174____

Jane Fiddyment Administratrix.

Letters Issued ____February 22,____ A. D. 19__1850__

C.L.Hewley

Clerk.

Fee Book _____ Page _____

ESTATE CLOSED

_____ 19 ____

Included in the estate were one spinning wheel, loom and appendage indicating that Elizabeth Jane was likely a "spinster" or one who spun wool into yarn. Note that "Letters issued February 22, 1850" is a court term and not relevant to the actual probate dates. The estate was closed in October of 1851.

Copy of original article reporting Walter Fiddyment's murder.

Horrible Tragedy.

A most shocking tragedy occurred in this town, on the 10th inst., which resulted in the death of Mr. Walter Feddyment, superintendent of Mr. Woodruff's distillery. We give a brief statement of the facts in this painful affair in order to correct the misrepresentations which are in circulation.

An altercation, about some trivial matter, took place between Mr. Feddyment and a man named Thomas Bwyn, in one of the rooms of the distillery. The latter using insulting language was ordered out of doors by the former, and on refusing to go, after some further quarrel, Mr. Feddyment put him out at the door. Bwyn returned again and Feddyment took hold of him the second time to put him out, when he stabbed Feddyment with a knife, in three defferent places in his abdomen, letting his intestines out, besides giving him several cuts on his arms and in his side. Feddyment, by the assistance of a man who was present, became disengaged and fled, but being pursued by Bwyn, notwithstanding his wounds, seized hold of a shovel, turned and dealt his pursuer such a blow as to fell him to the floor. After which he escaped into an adjoining room and fastened the door against his assailant. The person who was present in the affray, was so alarmed and excited that he ran for a physician, without giving the alarm to others about the establishment. Upon the arrival of the Physician and others at the scene, the victim was found lying on the floor in a state of insensibility. He was carried to his residence—his wounds were examined and pronounced mortal, and he lingered in the most excruciating agony until the following day, when he breathed his last. An inquest was held by Coroner Richards, after which Bwyn was arrested, and is confined in jail in this place, to await his trial at the next term of our Circuit Court. When doubtless he will be allowed a fair hearing.

Mr. Feddyment was a young man of sober, temperate and industrious habits, and was highly esteemed in this community. He leaves a wife and child and other relatives to mourn his sad fate; as well as a large circle of friends who regret his untimely and melancholy end. Bwyn resided about three miles south of this place—has a wife and two children, is said to be a man of steady habits, and up to the time of the unfortunate event detailed above, we learn, was on intimate terms with Feddyment. Truly, he that controleth his own temper is greater than he that taketh a city.

2

Gold Fever

Before Jane and Walter were married in 1850, gold fever began sweeping the world. On December 5, 1848, President James Polk made the formal announcement that California was a gold-rich land. Once the news was official, people all over America urgently formed groups to make the journey west.

Early in 1849 an ad in the Lockport, Illinois newspaper publicized that a number of locals were forming "The Lockport Group" with the intention of traveling overland to the gold fields. Four leading members of this group included Armstead Runyon and his three eldest sons.

Armstead was Jane's brother-in-law, married to her sister, Mary. The families lived near each other and Jane and her sister Mary were close.

Armstead had a plan. He knew that California was a land he wanted to explore, and he also knew that time was of the essence. There would be thousands heading west, and if he was to have any success he had to be one of the first to arrive. His three eldest sons* would be good companions for the long overland journey, and together they could determine if there was value in California, gold or otherwise.

Once the Lockport Group was formed, Armstead was one of its main leaders. The group of men pooled their resources, organized themselves into a business venture, and headed to California.

On the day Armstead left for California, he promised his wife Mary and their children that they would all make the journey to move west only if it was truly worth the long and dangerous trip.

In the spring of 1849 the 10 members of the Lockport Group set out. They reached the Missouri "jumping-off point" of St. Joseph in good order and, along with hundreds of other groups, readied themselves for the long overland trek ahead.

Armstead and his three sons were on their way to California. His young wife, Mary Crawford Runyon, and their two small children were left

ST. LOUIS REPUBLICAN

APRIL 19, 1849

In addition to the companies from Illinois, previously noticed, the following are in the field, and ready to move from Will County, and composed of

Kercheval, A.F.

Mahoney, David

Mahoney, John

Newton, J.W.

Parks, William

Runyon, A.N.

Runyon, O.R. and A.

Runyan, S.

Rutherford, R.

would tend to the work of finishing their day's journey and after supper they would prepare themselves for sleeping. They either pitched tents or made their beds under the stars. Each night men took turns keeping watch.

Weeks turned into months on the trail and food would often become scarce. Cattle died under intense pressure and other parties abandoned their hopes and turned back. But the Lockport Group forged on, and after six long months of traveling the dusty trails they successfully reached California.

At first Armstead wrote letters home that spoke of gold. But this account became very brief, as it didn't take his group very long to move on and make their way to the Sacramento River. The letters explained that they had found the laborious and dangerous work of gold panning not as promising as the land. The area along the Sacramento River, on the Delta, looked especially good for farming. Armstead reported that he bought a ranch with 160 acres on Schoolcraft Island (now Sutter Island), at the head of what was called Steamboat Slough.

Time passed quickly and several years of farming and ranching in California convinced Armstead that this was the place for his family. He could see a prosperous future, and he knew

to wait at home in Illinois to anticipate and hope for Armstead's safe return.

The journey was long and treacherous. Along with thousands of other Argonauts, the group forged territory with sketchy maps and word-of-mouth information as their only guides. At dusk the wagons were circled up around the group to form a barrier between them-selves and any attackers. The weary travelers

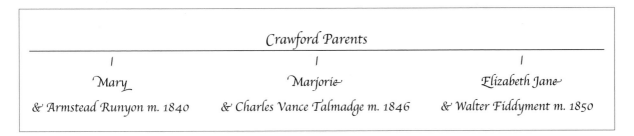

Crawford Parents		
Mary	*Marjorie*	*Elizabeth Jane*
& Armstead Runyon m. 1840	*& Charles Vance Talmadge m. 1846*	*& Walter Fiddyment m. 1850*

note: The family uses both "Marjorie" and "Margery" as spellings of this name.

his family would thrive in this new land. It had been four years and he was anxious to bring Mary and the children west.

Armstead began his trip back to Illinois in the spring of 1853. But this time his journey was not overland; he could now afford to take a quicker, more expensive sea voyage.

The last half of his journey was recorded:

Ship: *Prometheus, departing from the port at San Juan Del Norte in Nicaragua*

Arriving in the port of New York on May 12, 1853.

Two weeks after the ship's arrival Armstead reached his home. His overjoyed wife rushed into his arms. ❧

Jane's brother-in-law, Armstead Runyon, was her sister Mary's husband.

**Armstead's three eldest sons, Alexander, age 12; Orin, age 15; and Solomon, age 20, were from a prior marriage.*

3

Looking West

It is doubtful that Jane and Walter were ever planning to go to California. Jane Crawford had married into one of the most well established families in the area. In 1851, the Fiddyment families in Lockport, Illinois were successful farmers and distillers, and they were quite involved in the community. With strong family connections and support, there really wasn't a reason to leave. But when Walter was murdered everything changed.

Jane became a different woman. She grew in character. Her sadness, her mourning, and her overwhelming grief and horror at watching her young husband die summoned strength she didn't know she had.

For the two years following Walter's death, Jane worked hard to get her life in order. But not surprisingly the young widow longed for a new start. By mid-spring of 1853 her sister Margery and her husband Charles Vance Talmadge began the journey west on the overland trail with their children in tow. A month later, her sister Mary's husband, Armstead Runyon, arrived home from living in California for the past three years. His stories about the new state were mesmerizing, and his enthusiasm

was contagious. The Runyon family planned to leave for California in the early fall and take the Panama route. Soon, both of Jane's sisters and their families would no longer live in Lockport.

Jane had a decision to make. She could stay and depend on the security and support of her deceased husband's wonderful family, or she could start fresh while being in the company of her sisters and their families. She chose her sisters.

In late October of 1853, Jane and baby Walter, along with Jane's sister Mary, her husband Armstead, and their two children, set off on their adventure. Jane said tearful goodbyes to the family she loved so well, and promised she would write and hopefully come back soon to visit. The little group then boarded a stagecoach bound for New York City. From the city, they boarded a steamer headed to the Isthmus of Panama. Once in Panama, they made the long and dangerous overland trek by mule caravan to the western Panama shore.

With the Panama trip complete, they embarked upon another steamer to San Francisco. The

Biographical Sketches of the Leading Men and Women of the County Who Have Been Identified With Its Growth and Development from the Early Days to the Present

BY WILLIAM L. WILLIS
HISTORIC RECORD COMPANY
LOS ANGELES, CALIFORNIA (1913)

Pg. 905

"Armstead Runyon, 'with his sons, O.R., A.N. and Solomon, left Illinois early in the spring of 1849 and followed the usual route of migration across the plains, arriving safely at Sacramento during the middle of September. It was his privilege to witness the memorable era of early Californian development, the rapid accession to the population, the admission of the state into the Union, the growth in wealth from mines and of prosperity from the early expansion of agricultural interests, and with his own past experience amid frontier conditions he was in a position to understand and appreciate the environment of the period as well as the prospects for future development.'"

party arrived in California about mid December of 1853. The remainder of the trip was by boat through the San Francisco Bay and onto the Sacramento River — a 12-hour voyage. Their destination, Schoolcraft Island, lay 20 miles south of Sacramento at a beautiful spot in the Delta known as the head of Steamboat Slough.

The new ranch that Armstead and his sons had acquired was a wonderful sight. The total journey to California had been nearly two months, and once they were settled into their new home, it became obvious that traveling back to Illinois anytime soon was out of the question. Jane and baby Walter were weary from their travels but found relief on the peaceful property. Jane and her sisters were reunited; her new life had officially begun. ◦◦

ABOUT ARMSTEAD RUNYON AND EARLY SACRAMENTO

The Runyon property was strategically situated on the Sacramento River and was one of the best agriculturally producing ranches on the Delta.

– EXCERPT FROM HISTORY OF SACRAMENTO COUNTY CALIFORNIA

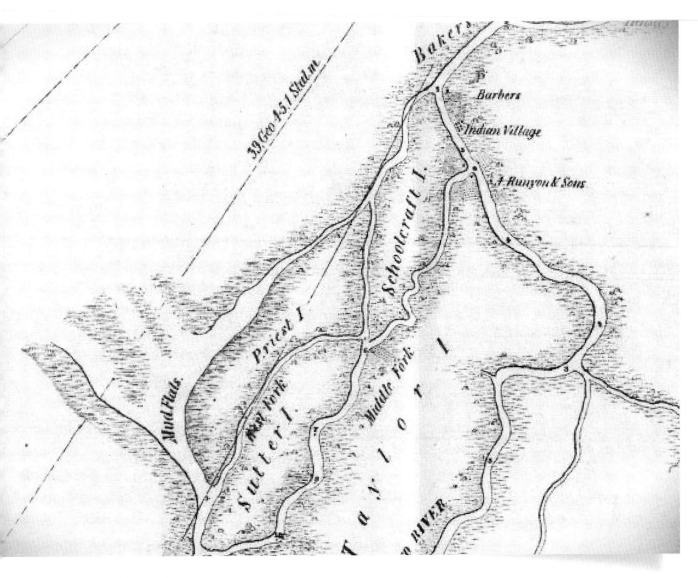

*Drawing of Steamboat
Slough, early 1850s.*

*Armstead Runyon and his sons
settled on the river within a year
of their fall 1849 arrival.*

4

A New Home A New Life

What a time to be in California! In 1854 the Runyons had already established a great orchard along the Sacramento River and were rapidly becoming the most prominent fruit growers in the area. Jane had the benefit of seeing her sister's family succeed — and this added to her courage and determination to establish her own life. She became optimistic about her future though she was certainly homesick for the Illinois countryside.

Jane's older sister Margery and her family had made it safely to California. She and her husband were also pursuing agricultural ventures. It was her two sisters and their connections that gave the young widowed mother the support and encouragement she needed.

In 1855, Charles Vance Talmadge, Jane's brother-in-law (Margery's husband) in exchange for a debt he owed her offered Jane land that he had acquired. What he was offering was located in the valley, north of Sacramento. The area was covered with wild grass and great oak trees. To Jane it was a lush countryside and she loved it. The area reminded her so much of Illinois and the

beautiful countryside she left behind, that she accepted the offer and hoped to eventually settle on this land.

Soon after the land transaction Jane married the new love of her life, George Hill. George was a brick mason by trade, but at heart he was a rancher and a farmer. The union of the two couldn't have been a better match. Young Walter now had a loving stepfather to help guide him into his early childhood, and Jane could pursue her life's new adventures with a loving partner.

The couple had their first child, Martha Frances, on November 23, 1855. Early the next year the young family took advantage of the land Jane had acquired and moved into a new home. They were in the Northern Sacramento Valley, called the Pleasant Grove District in Placer County. Their ranching days had begun, and the young couple was expecting another child. Their surprise must have been great as they discovered that their family was advancing by two! Twin boys, James and John, were born in Placer County on November 20, 1856. The family was now a group of six.

Throughout the next several years Jane and George increased their property holdings to total over 5,000 acres. Including the land they built their ranch on, they also acquired 2,800 acres of rangeland near Cisco, Placer County. This countryside was where they grazed their sheep and cattle during the summer months. They also bought 1,000 acres west of Lincoln, Placer County, and over 250 acres on the Sacramento River near Walnut Grove. Another area where they acquired 900 acres was then known as the "chaparral area" now mainly Granite Bay. They paid about a dollar an acre. ✍

5

Northern California in the Mid-19th Century

In the 1850's California was a state like no other. Its men were different and its women were even more different than the rest of America. The laws, customs, and protocol of the rest of the nation didn't apply here, and consequently it was a high-spirited place in a time that would be like no other. People were migrating to northern California by the thousands and were mostly intent on making their fortunes.

More than 200,000 Argonauts arrived. The majority of them went straight to the "diggings" and the earliest miners made the easiest money. In some places, incredibly, gold was lying on the ground just waiting to be picked up. Along river banks the lucky early miners dipped in their pans and swilled out thousands of dollars of the glistening metal. But their good fortune attracted a rush of people, and before long the easy gold was gone.

In this era fortunes were widely available and gold wasn't the only way. Food, shelter, and supplies quickly became scarce. The little village of 150 people that made up Sacramento in

April of 1849 had exploded into a small city of 6,000 by October of that same year. Everything was in short supply. Store keepers could name their price and get it.

At the height of the Gold Rush, a loaf of bread that cost 4 cents in the east sold for 75 cents in the mines. As much as $5 could be gotten for an egg, and $4 for an apple. With the average miner making $8 a day, most of their hard-earned money was spent just to survive.

Along with storekeepers, ranchers and farmers made handsome profits. Grain was grown and barley and oats were sold to teamsters who would haul the goods to the mining camps to sell. Local mill owners purchased wheat, milled it into flour, and then sold it at a high price to local cooks who were making their own fortunes selling their fare to the hungry miners. Cattle raised in the valleys were herded into Sacramento to be sold to butchers, who again sold the cut meat at enormous prices.

California fruit advertising was very popular in the mid-19th century.

As quickly as the lucky miner held gold in his hand, another hand was at the ready to sell him goods. After five or six months of back-breaking work in a cold stream bed, cooking over a campfire, and sleeping in a tent or little more than a shack, a prosperous miner was easily persuaded to buy several nights in a hotel with a soft bed, warm food, and plenty of liquor to wash it all down. If he was so inclined, he could easily buy female companionship. The charges were almost always exorbitant but the miners who could were more than happy to pay the price. ❧

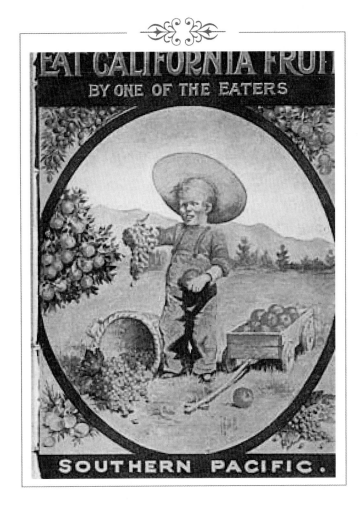

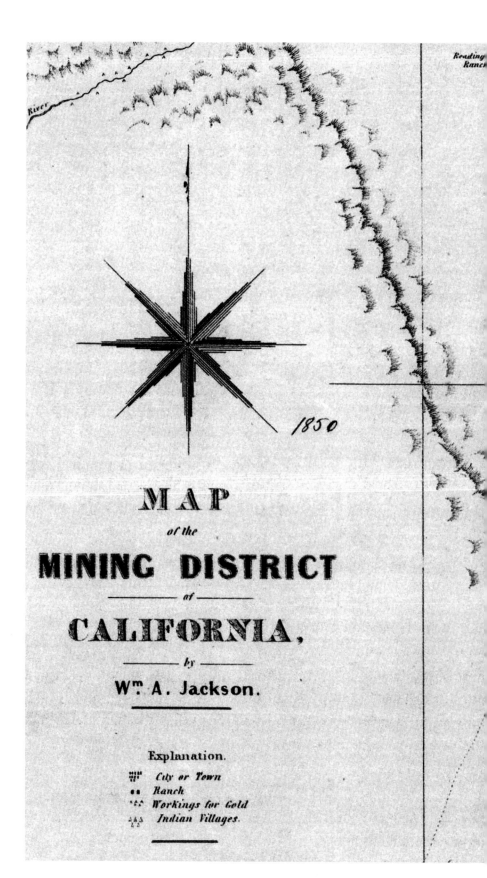

This 1850 mining map illustrates the unusual mix of people living in this section of the Placer County mining district.

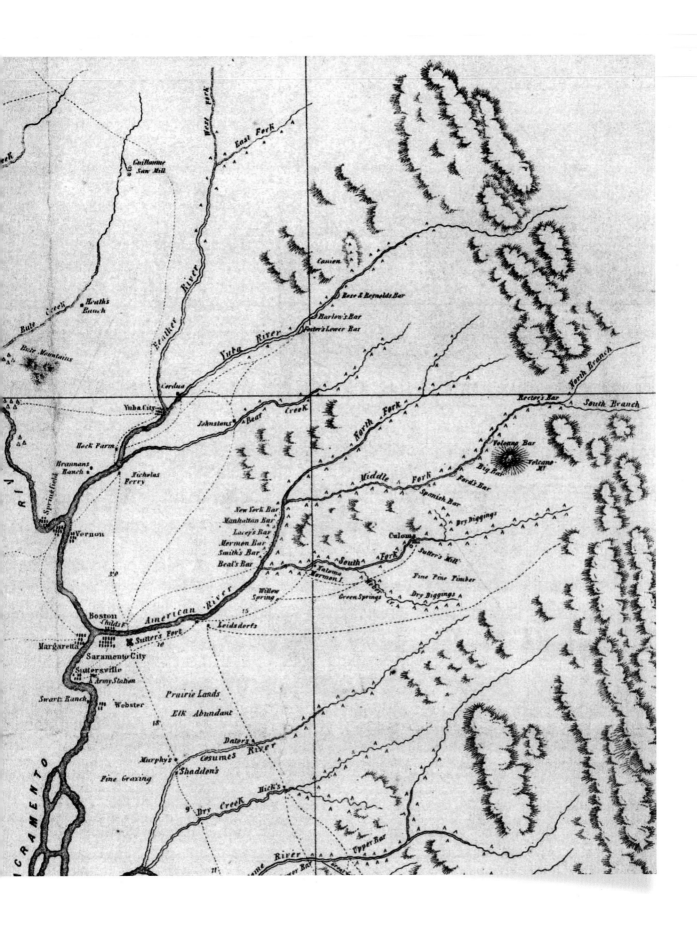

West Fork

East Fork

Guillarine
Saw Mill

Canion

Rose & Reynolds Bar

Heath's
Ranch

Butte Creek

Feather River

Yuba River

Barlow's Bar

Foster's Lower Bar

Bear Mountains

Cordua

North Branch

Yuba City

Rector's Bar

South Branch

Johnstons

Bear Creek

North Fork

Hock Farm

Volcano Bar

Big Bar

Volcano Mt

Brannans
Ranch

Nicholas
Ferry

Middle Fork

Springfield

Ford's Bar

Spanish Bar

Dry Diggings

New York Bar

Manhattan Bar

Vernon

Lacey's Bar

Columa

Mormon Bar

Smith's Bar

Sutter's Mill

South Fork

Beal's Bar

Yaloma
Mormon I.

Fine Pine Timber

Willow
Spring

Dry Diggings

Green Springs

American River

Boston
Childs F.

Leidsdorfs

Margareta

Sutter's Fort

Saramento City

Suttersville

Army Station

Swart: Ranch

Webster

Prairie Lands

Elk Abundant

Dators

Cosumes River

Murphy's

Shaddon's

Fine Grazing

Hick's

SACRAMENTO

Dry Creek

Upper Bar

River

6

David Tells the Story of Elizabeth Jane

David grew up hearing the tales of his earliest ancestor, Elizabeth Jane (a.k.a. Jane). He said from what he knew, he could surmise that Jane had realized that once her husband died, there really wasn't much in Illinois for her, so she decided to make the move to California. Once she came to California she stayed a little while with her sister, but she was an independent and enthusiastic woman. She began to expand her own sphere of influence in the area. She eventually got to know a particular man by the name of George Hill. He was a Sacramento merchant, and she fell in love and married him.

David goes on to tell that before or about the same time as the marriage, Jane's sister's husband, Charles Vance Talmadge, had apparently borrowed money from her. He either couldn't pay it back or didn't want to pay it back, and for the repayment he offered her land for his debt. He had 80 acres of land in Placer County, and this was only a year or two after California became a state in the Union.

Jane came up and looked it over. When she saw the area the land reminded Jane of Illinois so she decided to take the deal. She and her husband settled on the property and eventually had five children together. They built a cabin on the property and some speculate that old maps designated with "Hill Cabin" is the original cabin site of Jane and her husband.

They began to buy property in the area. She used the land for cattle farming and growing crops, and they made a better-than-average living. She had surplus cash from crops, cattle and maybe some grain. She kept buying property. Real estate was in abundance. Most property at that time was owned by would-be miners who were not successful in mining and had instead homesteaded the land. She began to buy up these homestead properties.

David remembers that there were wells all over the ranch. The Homestead Act required that to homestead a property a well and cabin had to be built. The person who was a homesteader had to build a cabin and had to get enough

Elizabeth Jane Crawford Fiddyment Hill Atkinson was the original Fiddyment pioneer in California.

from the land to support himself. These were hand-dug wells – and in the summer time the area was basically like a desert. The wells proved the homesteader was using the land. The wells varied from 12 to 25 feet deep and most were brick-lined. This was the primary water source to the homesteaders.

The value of the land at that time was around $1 per acre. One early family transaction shows land was sold at $280 for 360 acres.

David completed his recollection, stating that Jane also bought land in the local foothills and mountains where she ranged her cattle. Cattle ranging land was important and at that time the federal government didn't have organized forested land. She also owned land on the Sacramento River. By the time she passed away (in 1906), her estate was over 16,000 accumulated acres. ❧

Elizabeth Jane Crawford

& Walter Fiddyment m. 1850	& George Hill m. 1855	& Ashby Atkinson m. 1868
		[no children]
Walter	Martha	
	James	
	John	
	Frank	
	Georgia	

7

Walter Fiddyment
The Pleasant Grove District

In 1861 young Walter Fiddyment could stand on the highest point of his family's land and see snowcapped Sierra-Nevada Mountains to the east, the coast mountain range to the west, and endless acres of his ranch all around him. On his land grew miles of long groups of oak, sycamore and cottonwood trees. Between these massive tree groves sat rolling green valleys with cattle roaming and feeding upon lush grasses that grew there. A deep, crystal-clear creek ran through the property, and from this waterway fingers of seasonal streams and brooks branched out to provide water for the cattle and grain crops. The closest neighbor was over 200 acres away.

In those days it all seemed idyllic. For five years the ranch had been their home and his mother and new father were doing well together. The family business of raising cattle and growing grain crops was increasingly profitable. With hundreds of miners in the surrounding area, and towns forming throughout the county, cattle and grain

were commanding high prices. Walter now had four siblings, sister Martha, twin brothers James and John, and the youngest, four-year-old Frank. He would soon have a new baby in the family as his mother was pregnant once again. The family was growing and their livelihood with the land was proving to be a success.

Even though he was just 10-years old, Walter was quickly learning the ranch operations. He didn't remember Illinois or much about the details of the move west with his mother; all he ever really knew was California. His mother taught him a basic academic education, but his stepfather taught him to be a rancher. Day after day, Walter and George Hill worked side by side to tend to the hard work of living off the land.

The young boy was thriving. His nearly 11-year-old frame was lean and strong. He had piercing blue eyes and thick dark hair. He was quite tall for his age, and he easily handled his chores on the ranch. Walter was growing

1860 CENSUS

Township 10, Placer County

George Hill, 31; Elizabeth Jane, 31

Walter [Fiddyment], 10

Martha, 5

James, 4

John, 4

Frank, 4

Real estate value $2000

Personal estate value $2800

up in an era like no other, on the western frontier in the middle of Gold Rush country.

With the success of the ranch and his mother's pending birth to another child, it would normally have been a time to celebrate. But trouble was on its way, and Walter and his mother were about to face yet another tragedy. ❧

1860 AGRICULTURAL SCHEDULE

George Hill

Acres of Land Improved 100

Acres of Land Unimproved 160

Cash Value of Farm $2000

Value of Farming Machinery $40

Horses 5

Milk Cows 40

Other Cattle 60

Sheep 10

Swine 75

Value of Livestock $2150

Bushels of Wheat 300

Bushels of Barley 400 (used to feed animals)

Lbs of Butter 800

Tons of Hay 5

Value of Home Made Manufacture $240

Value of Animals Slaughtered $100

8

Turmoil Strikes and A Baby is Born

The end of summer in the Pleasant Grove District of Placer County is often nothing short of miserable. It is the time that rain hasn't fallen for four, sometimes five months. Temperatures are easily in the 90's for many days, sometimes reaching over 100. The earth is scorched. The rancher has his cattle in the nearby foothills. Family food sources are from storage and any end-of-summer garden vegetables are those that have been kept alive from well water. A family letter written on September 2 reported:

"The weather is all most unendurable, it looks as though the world is on fire, no wind to speak of, hot night and day … the hogs are seethering all around the country."
– Walter Fiddyment

On September 3, 1861, Walter's world was made nearly intolerable when he received word that his stepfather had died. The only father he had ever known, his mother's husband of six years, and the father of his four siblings, was suddenly gone. The world he and his mother knew was once again hit with tragedy.

A bright spot in the midst of the miserable days was that Walter's mother gave birth to a beautiful baby girl in late September. In honor of her deceased husband, she named her baby Georgia. The infant was a joy in this dark time. But, the joy would soon be put on hold. In December, a great flood inundated Sacramento and the surrounding area.

Water reached inland for miles and miles. The city of Sacramento was only accessible by canoe. The flood came upon the area so quickly that there wasn't time to move any cattle. A majority of the family's cattle was being grazed on land outside of Sacramento and all were drowned. It was a major loss.

Walter's mother had experienced misfortune before, but her family's situation in early 1862 was extremely difficult. She had to stay strong and rely on the only person she could count on, her son.

Flooding on the ranch.

As many pioneer children did, Walter took on very adult responsibilities early on. Before he was 12-years old, he was becoming the main caretaker of his mother's ranch. His family was now comprised of his mother and five siblings all under the age of seven. ☙

9

The Iron Horse

From the time he was five-years old, Walter could hear the distant whistle of a giant locomotive*. When plans were made for the California Central** Railroad to run through his community, he could hardly contain his excitement.

He watched as men from all around joined in the enormous effort of grading the land. With their tools and teams of horses, they worked from sunup to sundown. As the ground was being prepared for the rails, discussion was high with anticipation about the changes to come.

Farmers and ranchers were accustomed to the two-plus days trip to haul their goods into Sacramento. With the railroad, grains, fruits and vegetables could be loaded locally. The laborious and long cattle drives would soon be shortened to a day's work as cattle could be weighed and shipped directly onto local freight cars. Life was about to get much easier on this western frontier!

All across the United States, people had great hopes for the possibilities that railroads created, and there were dreams that tracks would eventually span the distance of the country. Finally, with the backing of the federal government, the dream was to be realized. In Sacramento a new rail line was created called the Central Pacific, and it was destined to be the western half of America's new transcontinental railroad.***

Owned by Crocker & Company, the Central Pacific started in Sacramento and crossed the California Central rails at an area referred to as Junction. On April 26, 1864, the first passengers of the Central Pacific rode from Sacramento to Junction. From that day forward trains ran this route daily.

The Iron Horse was now running full speed through southwestern Placer County and with it came a new era of growth. Hundreds of new settlers rushed in to claim land throughout the rich agricultural region. As shipping and trading took hold, great possibilities evolved for a booming business economy. Passengers on the daily train watched as the area called Junction, once in the middle of nowhere, started to grow. Almost immediately a train depot was built. A hotel, pioneer store and blacksmith shop soon followed.

Technically the Gold Rush was still on, but now there were exciting new prospects. With the future in mind, on August 13, 1864, a town plat was laid out and the area called Junction was given the new name of Roseville. Progress was at hand and a real community was emerging.

In November of 1864, Walter wasn't quite old enough to vote but it was certain he would always remember that year's presidential election. The people of Roseville and vicinity cast 29 votes for the Republican candidate Abraham Lincoln, and 17 votes for the Democrat nominee General George McClellan. Those early settlers surely set the tone for the community's future elections. ࡐ

The Sacramento Valley Railroad ran from Sacramento to Folsom. Its trial run was August 17, 1855 and was the first railroad west of the Rockies.
**The California Central Railroad came from Folsom, the southeast, and eventually curved northwest. Its tracks reached Lincoln in 1861.*
***The first transcontinental railroad was completed on May 10, 1869 with the west and east rail lines meeting at Promontory Point, Utah.*

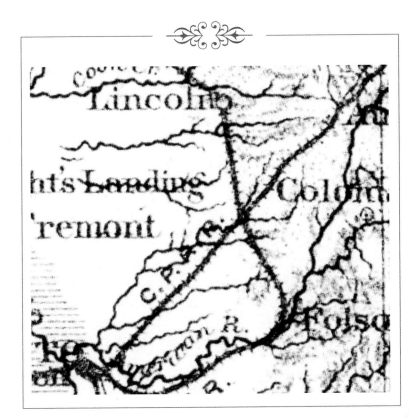

Early map showing the Central Pacific and California Central Railroad crossing; the place also known as Junction.

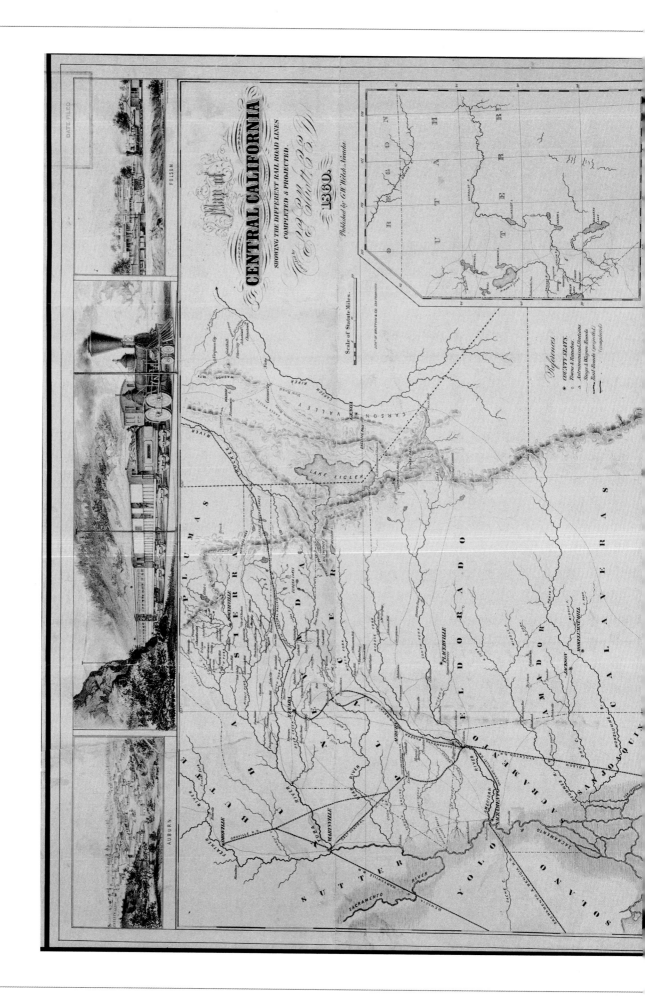

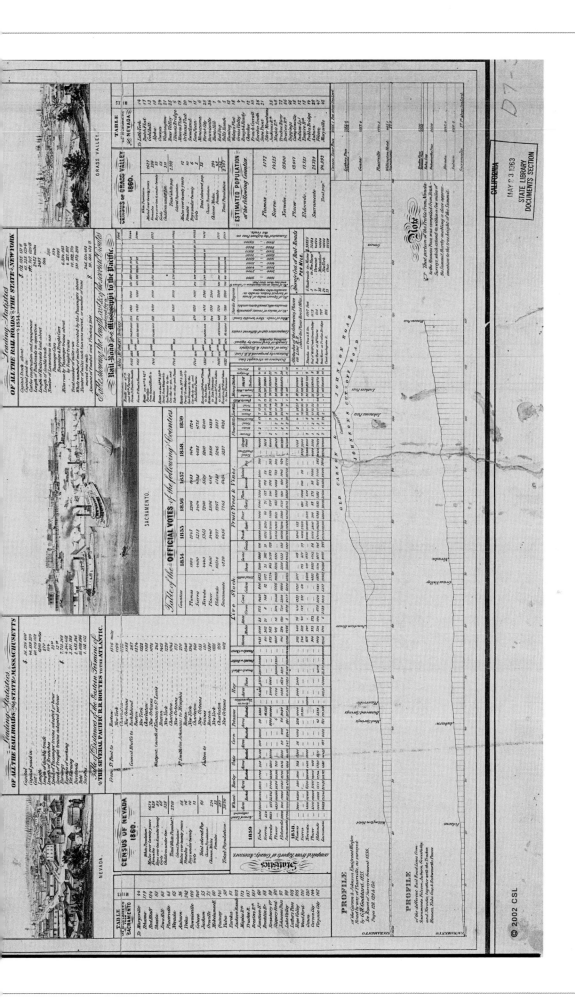

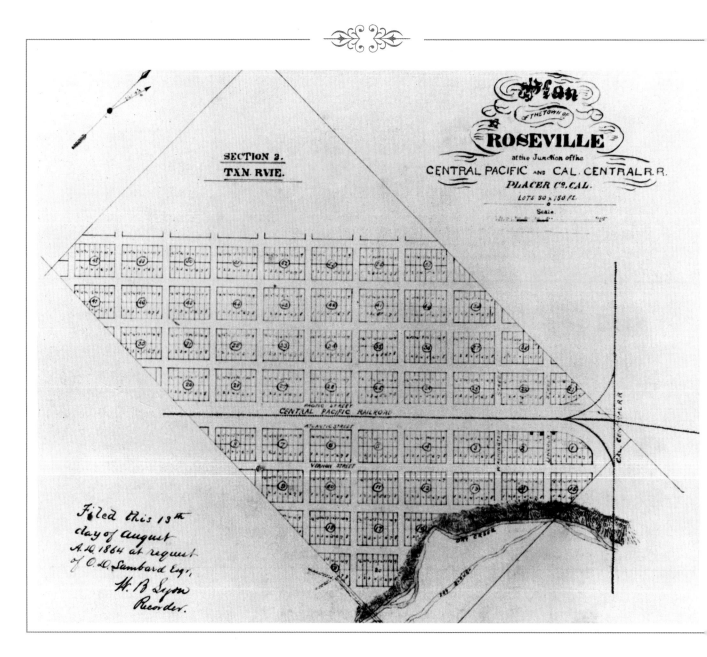

1864 map depicting the imagined city of Roseville.

10

The Ranch

As Roseville took shape, so did Walter's family ranch in the nearby Pleasant Grove District. In the 10 years spanning 1860 to 1869 his mother's real-estate holdings more than tripled, growing in worth from $2,000 to $6,750. Her personal estate also tripled, expanding in value from $2,800 to $8,500. Her 1000-plus acres of land holdings that began in the Pleasant Grove District, now reached to the Chaparral Region (Granite Bay) and included acreage in the foothills in the east, and more acreage in the west near the Sacramento River. Land was selling at $1 to $2 an acre.

As the Pleasant Grove District expanded, so did the families. With so many new children growing up in the area, the need for a school became apparent. Walter's mother had experienced firsthand the value of education and was deeply committed to children's academic learning. She generously donated an acre of land for a school house to be built, and on August 2, 1864, the Pleasant Grove School District was formed. Elizabeth Jane Hill (Walter's mother) was its first schoolteacher.

The one-room school house sat at the top of an oak-studded knoll with a stream flowing near the bottom of the hill. The school children nicknamed it Toad Hill School and classes ran continuously through 1880. The building also served as a Sunday school and later on, the adult Walter Fiddyment served as its teacher.

The smokehouse was an integral part of daily life on the Fiddyment ranch.

With the fundamentals of reading, writing and arithmetic in place, Walter and his mother continued to work side by side to expand their cattle ranch and improve their grain farming. Nearby Sacramento readily accepted these products, and Walter completed his education from his mother by learning how to compete in the business world.

Their success continued — and in the process his mother also taught Walter the importance of compassion. The area was growing but there was still a great lack of facilities. To help out, Walter's mother offered assistance with the sick and infirm. She also delivered babies when the occasion arose. It was common knowledge of the day that many of the district's children were delivered by "Aunt Jane."

In 1868, Walter's mother married a third time to Ashby Jones Atkinson. The couple remained together several years but no children were born of this union. Unfortunately it turned out to be a regretful relationship and in a move unprecedented for a woman of her day, Walter's mother filed in the courts to be the family's sole trader. Finally, in 1877, she filed for divorce. She would remain single for the rest of her life. ❧

THE DECADES OF THE 1860S AND 1870S WAS A REMARKABLE TIME IN OUR COUNTRY'S HISTORY. *The Civil War was being fought (1861-1865) while millions of dollars were being pumped into the Union economy from California mined gold. In 1869 transportation took a giant leap as the transcontinental railroad was completed. Thousands of miles of railroad track began to span the United States and people moved about accordingly.*

Yet there was no refrigeration, electric lamps or telephones. A good horse was invaluable, as was a double-barreled rifle and a Colt revolver. Barbed-wire fencing was introduced and the era of open-range cattle grazing and ranchers' feuds over grazing lands was ended.

By 1870, California agriculture promoters had outdone themselves. Would-be farmers arrived in northern California to discover that most of the acres suitable for dry-land farming were already occupied. The only option a new settler had was to buy a developed farm at an inflated cost. California farmers were quickly realizing that irrigation was the key to growth and the subject became a statewide concern.

Farmers in Pleasant Grove District were fortunate in that the underground water supply was plentiful. Deep wells were dug and used for irrigation all throughout the area. Walter was able to access irrigation water throughout his land. There was a wide stream with several tributaries along with many wells that had already been dug throughout the property. He was ideally situated for both cattle ranching and crop growing.

A family member's drawing of buildings on the Fiddyment land at the main ranch house.

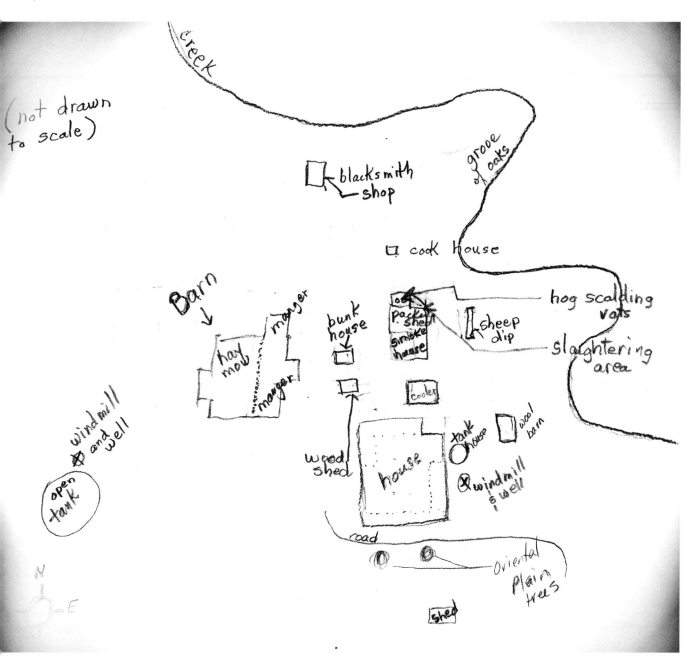

creek

(not drawn to scale)

blacksmith shop

grove of oaks

cook house

Barn

manger

hay mow

manger

bunk house

oak packing shed smoke house

hog scalding vats

sheep dip

Slaghtering area

windmill and well

open tank

wood shed

house

cooler

tank house

wool barn

windmill & well

road

Oriental Plain trees

shed

N

E

11

1879 Ella Bond

With time the ranch developed and expanded. Walter's siblings grew up and his mother became known as a leader in the concerns of local business and development. Walter was 28, still living at home and still single. Interests of the ranch took Walter to Elk Grove where he frequently did business, and in 1879 he found himself having caught the eye of a local businessman's daughter. The man's name was Augustus Bond and his daughter was Ella. Theirs was a destined relationship.

Ella Bond was a native Californian. Her father was a brick mason; an occupation that Walter deeply respected and was familiar with from his stepfather's teachings. Ella's mother, Frances Eustis Bond, was an immigrant from Illinois and the niece of Tamsen Donner, thus making Ella the great niece of Tamsen Donner.

Even though it had been over 30 years, people still talked about the tragedy in the mountains. Soon there was to be a new book published about the event, and it would surely contain exaggerated accounts of what really happened. Rumors were plentiful – and the family sometimes struggled with the weight of the idle gossip.

Ella was soon to be married and her mother took this time to have a serious discussion with her about their lineage.

The Donner Lineage

Ella's hands trembled as she picked up the small journal. Its pages were dog-eared and its leather cover felt soft and fragile on her fingers. She had heard rumor of this relic from the past, but until now she wasn't sure it actually existed. Written in her mother's handwriting, the inside back cover read, "On the 17th of March we left home in the year of 1852." The book's pages were filled with entries documenting her mother's overland trip to California.

The diary itself was symbolic of her mother's past. It was an heirloom being entrusted to her. Along with the diary, she would now learn the story of her mother's relationship with her Aunt Tamsen and the Donner family.

For as long as she could remember, Ella had heard stories about the tragedy in the mountains. There were many startling stories,

*A very young Ella Bond,
future wife of Walter Fiddyment.*

most of which had been fueled by poorly researched newspaper articles. Ella's mother refused to engage in the nonsense and now that her daughter was about to start her own family, it was important that she appreciate and protect this part of her heritage.

Frances began her family story by sharing with Ella that as a young girl, she very much wanted to accompany her Aunt Tamsen and family on their overland journey. It was because of

her father's insistence that she not go, that she chose to stay home in Illinois.

Frances explained that when she lived in Illinois she spent a great deal of her childhood in the company of her aunt. When Frances's own mother died, her father had sent for his sister, then a widow, to come to Illinois and live with them. Tamsen helped care for Frances and her siblings for many years. Eventually the roles reversed when Aunt Tamsen married

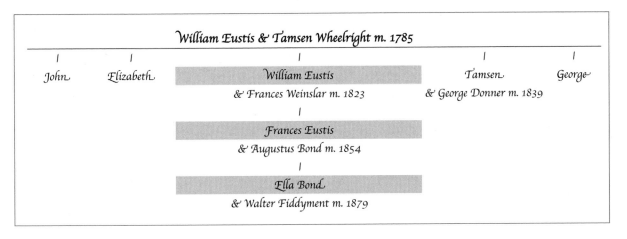

William Eustis & Tamsen Wheelright m. 1785

| John | Elizabeth | William Eustis & Frances Weinslar m. 1823 | Tamsen & George Donner m. 1839 | George |

Frances Eustis
& Augustus Bond m. 1854

Ella Bond
& Walter Fiddyment m. 1879

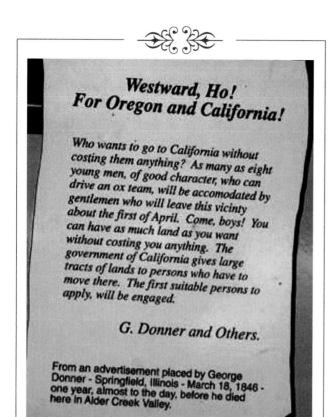

Westward, Ho!
For Oregon and California!

Who wants to go to California without costing them anything? As many as eight young men, of good character, who can drive an ox team, will be accomodated by gentlemen who will leave this vicinity about the first of April. Come, boys! You can have as much land as you want without costing you anything. The government of California gives large tracts of lands to persons who have to move there. The first suitable persons to apply, will be engaged.

G. Donner and Others.

From an advertisement placed by George Donner - Springfield, Illinois - March 18, 1846 - one year, almost to the day, before he died here in Alder Creek Valley.

George Donner and had children of her own. At that point, Frances became a great help to her aunt and caretaker of her three daughters.

Frances loved her aunt's little girls, cousins Frances, Georgia and Eliza Donner. She had taken care of them from infancy, and she would sorely miss their company. As preparations were finalized, Frances went with her aunt to help pick out glass beads for trading with the Indians, silks for the Spaniards for land trades, and calico to sew new dresses.

Stark reality set in the day that three large, white covered wagons arrived in their front yard. The wagons would carry provisions, belongings, and the entire family far away from their Illinois home. When those wagons appeared, her mother explained, the sadness in her heart overwhelmed her.

On April 15, 1846, the day of departure was upon them. After tearful embraces and promises to write, heavy hearts gathered about the Illinois homestead and waved goodbye to the Donners. There was hope and excitement for their new adventures, but friends and relatives would miss this wonderful family.

Frances went on to explain that in the early months after their departure, correspondence from her aunt was steady. The letters were filled with descriptions of the countryside, events of their journey, and anticipation about their future in California. But her last letter told that there would not be correspondence for a while. Aunt Tamsen wrote that they had chosen to take a new route, and there would be no outposts for mail to be sent. Frances waited. By October, when the party should have reached their new home, there was still silence. No one knew what had happened to the Donners.

It was rare for Ella's mother to show tears, but relating her anguish over her missing aunt and family was a very tender memory. With sadness, she told Ella how she and her anxious relatives waited throughout the winter for word of the travelers. Then finally, in the early months of 1847 an article that had appeared in a Yerba Buena (San Francisco) newspaper was picked up in the States. The article described how a group of overland travelers had become stranded in the California mountains.

The news brought so many questions. Perhaps her aunt and family had been found. But if these were her people, would they be rescued?

FRANCIS EUSTIS BOND DIARY ENTRY:

18 Aug 1852

"Bode adieu to the city of the Saints & recommenced our journey onward to the land of gold. Our way is along the valley of the great Salt Lake. Came about 20 miles & camped in a Mormon settlement on a small stream. After tea, dancing was proposed and all seemed to be in favor of passing a few hours in that pleasant amusement. Water & musk melons for dessert."

-diary of Francis Eustis [Bond]

The article said the group needed immediate help. Had any of them died? Were her little cousins okay?

Frances's father, William Eustis, was the one who gave her the terrible news. Aunt Tamsen and Uncle George had died in the mountains, and many others had also perished. But there was a bit of hope relayed; it was believed that her cousins had lived. The exact whereabouts of the girls were unknown, but there was rumor that they had been adopted. Her father also took the opportunity to reaffirm that she should not travel west until the route was made safer.

The stories of the Donner party and their episode in the mountains were a shock to the nation. Frances heard some of the horrific tales even in Illinois. In 1849 her Aunt Elizabeth, Tamsen's sister, sent a letter to the California governor requesting that the Donner girls be found and sent back to the States. But by this time it was confirmed that the girls had been in the continuing care of a new family, and they wished to stay. It would be several more years before Frances and her cousins could be reunited.

The diary Ella held in her hands was the recording of her mother's 1852 journey west. All along the way her worried father wrote letters that were meant to reach her at designated outposts. His angst was made worse on those occasions when letters were returned to him unopened. Her mother's journey was relatively uneventful, but after the tragic events her family had experienced, Ella realized just how much courage it took for her to make the trip.

In the diary it is recorded that Frances reached the city of Sacramento in September of 1852. She was anxious to find her Donner cousins and eventually did so. Once they were reconnected, she spoke to them of their family in the east and encouraged the young girls to try to forget what had happened in the mountains.

Frances, in her steadfast way, relayed to Ella that it was always more important to look to the future rather than dwell on the past. While the family history was indeed a national event, Frances encouraged her daughter to avoid any discussion about the sensational stories.

Ella very much appreciated her mother's wisdom. To her family, the Donner story was much deeper than the tragedy in the mountains. Ella gained a great respect for the love

YERBA BUENA (SAN FRANCISCO) NEWSPAPER

THE STAR

January 16, 1847

Emigrants In The Mountains

It is probably not generally known to the people that there is now in the California mountains, in a most distressing situation, a party of emigrants from the United States, who were prevented from crossing the mountains by an early, heavy fall of snow. The party consists of about sixty persons – men, women, and children. They were almost entirely out of provisions when they reached the foot of the mountains, and but the timely succor afforded them by Capt. J.A. Sutter, one of the most humane and liberal men in California, they must have all perished in a few days. Capt. Sutter, as soon as he ascertained their situation, sent five mules loaded with provisions to them, but they found the mountains impassable in consequence of the snow. We hope that our citizens will do something for the relief of these unfortunate people.

YERBA BUENA (SAN FRANCISCO) NEWSPAPER

THE STAR

February 6, 1847

Company Left

A company of twenty men left here on Sunday last for the California mountains, with provisions, clothing, etc. for the suffering emigrants now there. The citizens of this place subscribed about $1,500 for their relief, which was expended for such articles as the emigrants would be most likely to need. Mr. Greenwood, an old mountaineer, went with the company as pilot. If it is possible to cross the mountains, they will get to the emigrants in time to save them.

and loss her mother had experienced. She hugged her dear mother and was thankful that someday she could share the diary's contents with her own family.

As she stored the little book away for safekeeping, Ella smiled as the thought of Walter and their upcoming nuptials came to mind. As her mother said, it was time to look forward.

"My sweetest privilege was an occasional visit to cousin Francis Bond, my mother's niece, who, with her husband and child, had settled on a farm about 12 miles from us. She also had grown up a motherless girl, but had spent a part of her young lady-hood at our home in Illinois. She had helped my mother to prepare for our long journey and would have crossed the plains with us had her father granted her wish. She was particularly fond of us "three little ones" whom she had caressed in babyhood. She related many pleasing incidents connected with those days, and spoke feelingly, yet guardedly, of our experiences in the mountains … I gathered counsel and comfort from the lips of that sympathetic cousin, and loved her word pictures of the home where I was born."
– Eliza Donner from her book "The Expedition of the Donner Party"

Eliza Donner Houghton writing to
cousin Frances Bond.

Elk Grove, Mar. 30, '79

Dear Cousin
            Your letter of 7ᵗʰ inst. was
quite a surprise was truly glad to hear
from you again — am sorry I could
not comply with your request sooner
will answer your questions as correctly
as I can remember
Question 1ˢᵗ Your mother's father's name
was William Eustis — her mother's name
Tamzine Wheelwright.
2ⁿᵈ Was born in Newberryport — Mass
3ʳᵈ Educated in same place com-
menced teaching when 15 years of age.
She taught all the higher branches of
Mathematics — Surveying — Geometry &c
was one of the best teachers.
4ᵗʰ Was born in 1801.
5ᵗʰ Do not know what their occupatio
were. I only know that the Wheelwrights
were well off and were considered a-
mong the first in Newberryport.
6ᵗʰ Reading Fremont's and Hastings
travels among the Rocky Mts. through
Oregon and California first induced
your father and mother to think of

I will say good-bye your Cousin
                                    F. E. Bond

This historically revealing letter between between Tamsen [nee Eustis] and George Donner's daughters Eliza and Georgia was written in January of 1894. At the time of the entrapment in the winter of 1846/47 Eliza was the youngest at 3 years old, Georgia was 4, and Frances was 6.

St John Wash Jan 22/1894

My dear sister & family:

Both of your letters are full of comfort "Our Heavenly father has bound your hearts with loving care, and blessed you with the reward of faithful servants, You start out so bravely to face the sorrows that come to meet you, willing to be used as instruments in His hand Over looking none of the blessings measured out to you, Reaching out helping hands to others who in weakness stumble while trying to gain footing in the right way — Eliza God has chosen you to act many hard parts, I am thinking about the time" When Keseberge was bending over the bed with arms out stretched saying Eliza you will sleep with me to night" Frances holds her little hands tighter clasping, You nestle close against her bosom while she speaks "No! You want to kill her." I have always believed that your life was spared by her efforts for he walked away as if over come by the words and actions and you seemed to realize that you had made a narrow escape, She would not allow you out of her sight "While awake We filled her heart and mind. Perhaps you do not remember the pantelet she was

Eliza, God has chosen you to act many hard parts. I am thinking about the time when Keseberg was bending over the bed with arms out stretched saying "Eliza you will sleep with me tonight." Frances holds her little hands tighter clasping. You nestle close against her bosom while she speaks "No you want to kill her." I have always believed that your life was spared by her efforts for he walked away as if over come by the words and actions and you seemed to realize that you had made a narrow escape.

Long Beach Cal,
April 16, 1899.

My Dear Cousin:—
You do not write but still we have something to keep you pleasantly in our thoughts. The five quince plants that you sent to Mr Houghton are doing finely and he is very proud of them.

We all have a special fondness for them on account of the associations connected with their mother plant, which come from our old home, and was carried away by you after that

"it to "405 Bullard Block, Los Angeles, Cal;"⁴

affectionately your cousin
Eliza P. Houghton

12

Walter and Ella Set Up House

Every acre was familiar to him. He knew the soil, the waterways, the best areas to graze cattle, and even how to access the secret places where deer and coyote hid their families from view. Walter was a nature lover and a natural explorer. He enjoyed walks through the groves of oak, cottonwood and pine. He especially loved the seasons of color when wild roses grew profuse along the streams, and some of his fields were fully carpeted in orange and purple blooms from the wild poppies and fragrant lavender.

When the time came to choose a place for his own, he picked his favorite acreage in the Pleasant Grove District. It was near the spot where his mother and late stepfather had set up their first home. The prized acreage, ideally situated just south of the creek, had been in his family for 20 years. With a small cabin and well already dug, Walter's land would provide a good beginning for his new life.

With the help of his father-in-law, a master mason, a new brick foundation was laid, a ground-floor structure was built, and the old cabin was raised up over the new structure to create a two-story house. Brick fireplaces were constructed at each gable end of the home, and

a small cookhouse was built in the back. To ensure they were entirely self-sufficient, a brick smokehouse, cooler, and large circular water reservoir were also added to the property.

The 10'x10' smokehouse had to be built with extreme precision if the meat was to be properly smoked. Smoke from a fire would be built on the ground inside the building and had to be efficiently vented through the top. To do this small wood-lined vent holes, one centered on each side, were created near the roofline of the two-story brick structure. Each vent hole had hand-hammered hinges that supported wooden coverings so airflow could be regulated during the smoking process.

Next to the smokehouse a slaughterhouse was built so that animal food preparation could be contained to this area. Outside of the slaughterhouse, an underground pit was dug and a grate was installed over the top, which created a much-needed blood reservoir. Hogs also required further preparation as they had to be scalded in kettles, so their skin and hair could be removed. Once this initial process was complete, the meat could be smoked. Depending upon the meat, the entire exercise

Walter Fiddyment dressed in his Sunday best. Early 1890's.

took several days to a week's time to complete. Once smoked, meat could be stored but it had to be at a cool temperature.

To accommodate meat and other food goods, an 8' x 8' cooler was built. Its brick walls were built 12-inches deep, along with two kitty-corner windows complete with thick wood-shutter coverings. At night the shutters were opened so cool air could envelope the inside of the structure, then at daybreak the coverings were shut tight to keep the hot air out and the cool air in. Along its interior walls shelves and cabinets were installed so the family could keep food that needed to be stored at lower temperatures. Along with the smoked meat, this included a great many jarred fruits and vegetables. The cooler served as a food storehouse and was especially crucial during winter months when food was otherwise scarce.

Southwest of the main house where the land curves gently upward, a circular brick reservoir was created. It was 30 feet in diameter, about six feet tall, and 18- to 24-inches thick. The top of the reservoir extended about 1 ½ to 2 feet above the ground. A nearby well provided water, and a windmill was installed so the water could be pumped into the reservoir. Its main purpose was for watering the livestock but over the years the family would use it and lovingly refer to it as "the tank."

Windmills provided an important function to early ranchers. Walter installed several, including one over the well next to his new house. The water from this well was pumped into a tank that was built atop the cooler. The tank was positioned so that its height was above the house so water could easily be run from the tank into the house. In this way the Fiddyment home was one of the earliest in the area to have the attributes of running water.

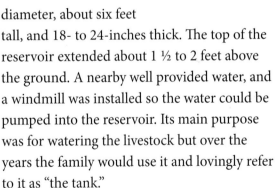

Walter Fiddyment & Ella Bond m. 1879

|

Ira

Frank

Mabel

Russell

Marjorie

Florence

The Fiddyment ranch house as it was first built. A cabin was raised to serve as the second story while a new addition was built for the first floor. c.1890 Walter stands in his front yard with his two dogs and presumably two of his children.

A blacksmith shop was created for any iron works needed. Ranch hands went to the blacksmith for everything from hooks needed in the smokehouse, to horseshoes and simple machinery repair. The blacksmith shop was yet another critical component of the ranch and its ability to operate independently.

A barn was constructed early on to accommodate grain farming, and eventually a separate wool barn was built to accommodate the shearing of the sheep. As their cattle investment grew, a manger area was added to the main barn to ensure lambing was well supervised.

Over the years thousands of sheep would be ushered through this barn. As the animals were herded through it was an opportunity to tend to their needs, especially if there were babies or pregnant mothers. If a ewe were pregnant she could be taken care of, or if a mother were separated from her lamb ranch hands could reunite the two. It wasn't unheard of that competing ewes would try to steal a baby. If that occurred, the baby lamb was in danger of dying since the accomplice usually wouldn't be a lactating mom. Keeping the babies warm, and ensuring they could nurse from their mothers, was a big part of lambing. Sheep mortality could be as high as 20 percent, and it was up to the ranch hands to be good caretakers to keep mother and babies as healthy as possible.

The labor-heavy harvest season required that extra help be hired. During the harvest all of the family members would carry out extra chores. Workers often required four meals a day, and it was usually the women, or hired cooks if available, who would take turns being responsible for the meals. The pressure could be overwhelming.

Family correspondence provides a brief look into their lives during the long, hot days of the grain-hauling season.

"We are all most cooked. I don't believe I ever experienced such hot weather. We have just washed the dinner dishes for the threshers. They came here Saturday morning for breakfast and to day is the last meal for a while. We have 2 ½ days again sometime. We cooked for Fergurson, Mac Kinnow, and Eli. They have not threshed on the Whalz Place nor lower Ranch yet. They go to Mr. Leonardo for supper."

"We had the herders with the threshers until Monday noon, in fact we have had them all of the time. The grain all turned out better than ex-pected. When the ranch hands were gone or taken care of by another family, the work didn't stop.

"… it is warm work putting up fruit, I had all most rather go hungry than start a fire any more. – July 6, 1879 To Ella from Walter's sister, Mattie (Martha)

"The boys have been summer fallowing every day since we have been down yesterday. Up at half past 4 o'clock in the morning, running three teams."

As the years went by, Walter and Ella worked together every day at keeping their ranch productive and their family in good order. While the work was sometimes a monumental effort, there were days of celebration and family quiet times too. When those days occurred all involved could take time to enjoy this lovely spot in the Pleasant Grove District.

Standing at their backdoor, they could see the nearby creek meandering through thick groves of heritage oaks and forest-green pines. In the springtime, they walked the creek and gathered the poppies, lavender and wild roses to create colorful bouquets for their picnics. If they looked to the horizon they would see just their land, fields open and sprawling, set against the expanse of a deep blue sky. ❧

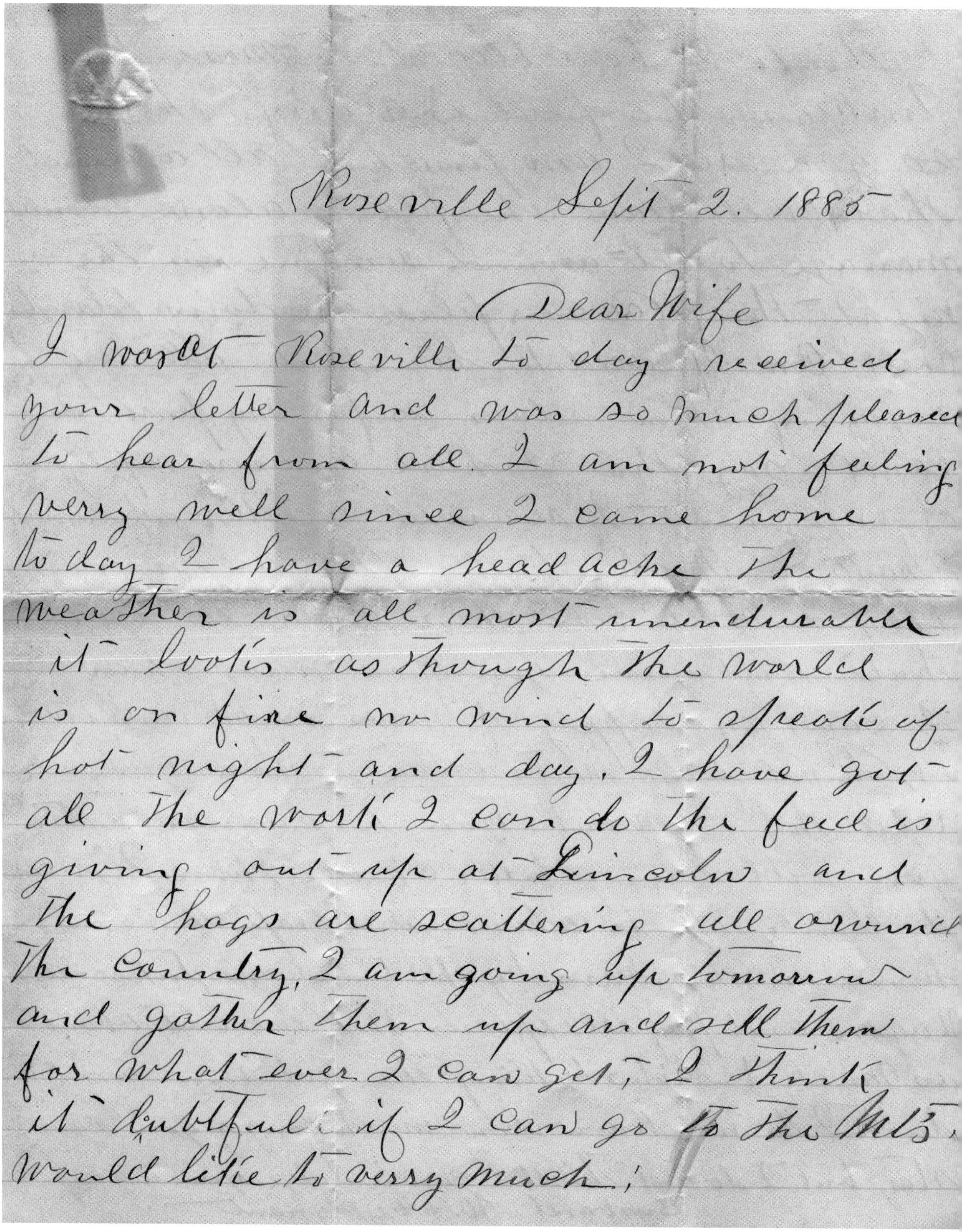

Roseville Sept 2. 1885

Dear Wife

I was at Roseville to day received
your letter and was so much pleased
to hear from all. I am not feeling
verry well since I came home
to day I have a head acke the
weather is all most unendurable
it looks as though the world
is on fire no wind to speak of
hot night and day, I have got
all the work I can do the fuel is
giving out up at Lincoln and
the hogs are scattering all around
the Country I am going up tomorrow
and gather them up and sell them
for what ever I can get, I think
it dubtful if I can go to the Mts
would like to verry much;

I think I will be obliged to move the
Turkeys the feed is getting short
so you see I am pinched all around
that will leave the places alone, I could
manage to get around somtine in the
Night. Things @ our place are doing tolarable
well am pleased to hear that all are
enjoying them selves as for my part I
Canot say that I have an over suply
of enjoyment I received a letter from
Matt & Mother to day they are in
Ill, I will send their letter to you
that will give you more news than
I can; My suply of news is at a low
eb, do not loose Matts letter, i When you
read the letter I want you to answer it
you will have a better Chance than I,
I think it is about as cheap to come
home on the cars, by the time one takes a
Wagon and pay all expenses they are out about
as much besides taking the hot sun and
dust, I do not Know how much longer you can
stay but I do not think I can indulge you a great
Husband W. F. Fiddyment

while longer love to all and kiss for the children you.

13

Living Near a Little Town

Walter's livelihood was a good choice for the latter half of the 19th century. His grain crops were profitable, his cattle were easily sold and used not only for their meat, but for their tallow and hides as well; the sheep he raised were invaluable for their wool. His eventual foray into the turkey business would prove to be a successful commodity not only for himself, but also for his sons' futures. Adding to his good fortune was his marriage into the Bond family.

Ella and Walter's half-sister, Martha, had been close friends for years and after the marriage the family ties grew even stronger. Whenever support was needed family members didn't hesitate to pitch in. Whether it was wheat threshing, lamb shearing, canning, or even assisting with the birth of a baby, helping hands could mean the difference between success and failure.

It was likely that Walter's mom, Elizabeth Jane, and Ella's mom, Francis Bond, both assisted with Ella's pregnancies and subsequent births. Over a 17-year period Ella would give birth to seven children, and six would survive. Their names in birth order: Ira Walter, in 1880; Francis "Frank" Augustus in 1882; Mabel E. in 1885; Russell Frederick in 1886; Marjorie E. in 1891; Albert

1895 (infant death); and Florence in 1897. They raised their family on the ranch and while they were self-sufficient, the nearby town had grown to include a few stores and was able to offer some goods that were not available on the ranch.

From Walter's ranch, Roseville was a little over seven miles, but it could be a longer trip depending on the weather and streams. Originally called "Junction" because of its location at the crossing of the Central Pacific and California Central railroads, Roseville had grown to be a shopping and trading center for the area farmers and ranchers. Wares were brought into the freight depot to be sold and shipped. While in town, customers could stop at one of the two pioneer stores to mail a letter, and perhaps buy or trade for some coffee and sugar. A blacksmith shop could offer repairs or new tools. If it were at the end of a work day rowdy shouts from the Roseville Hotel at the corner of Lincoln and Pacific streets might be heard as railroad workers shared a drink or two.

A block away from the hotel, Walter attended monthly Odd Fellows meetings in a new three-story brick building on Pacific Street. Also new to the town was a Presbyterian Church on Vernon Street and a Methodist Church at the corner

Walter Fiddyment with his Sunday school class posing in front of the school house his mother built. Early 1890's.

of Church and Washington streets. Walter's family attended Sunday services at the Presbyterian Church and as the years went by, they would become significant contributing members.

While the growth of Roseville offered a few conveniences, life was still very much contained on the ranch.

They churned their own butter:
"It has been raining here all day long and is now five o'clock and is all most dark. We churned to night and we thought it would never come it was so cold."
– November 29, 1879

The condition of their fields was constantly on their minds:
"I tell you the fields are looking nice. Hay is worth $17 a ton."
– Spring 1882

They wrote to each other about their work (cars refers to the railroad):
"Pa brought up a load and had the rest shipped on. The cars will be here Wednesday then he thinks he will be able to work a few days for Mrs. Hill."
– August 26, 1883

circa 1895 Walter and Ella Fiddyment take a family portrait with five of their children in front of the recently remodeled ranch house.

Left to right: Frank, Mabel, Walter holding Marjorie, Russell, Ella, Ira (Florence is not born yet).

They sewed their own clothes and sent patterns and clothing items to each other (a basque is a kind of jacket):

"… I got the pattern of those little drawers for Frankie, and I thought I would send them to you as I don't know when I will see you. I hope you will like them as they are just the thing for little fellows like him."
– August 24, 1884

"I made a comforter yesterday and day before."

"I finished your basque yesterday and nearly basted the sleeves in. If you have to cut out the arms don't rip only under the arms, and the neck I think will have to be cut out more. I was afraid I would spoil it and thought you had better try it on first. Think that collar will be too short and have made another one."
– February 25, 1887

As was common for the time, the boys learned to work on the ranch as soon as they could walk. The children referred to here are Ira, 5, and Frank, 3:

"The children are real good. Walter has them out with him the most of the time."
– February 18, 1885

Work on the ranch is laborious, and on the hottest of summer days it is miserable. Walter writes to Ella while she is away summering with family members in the cool mountains. He says he's not feeling well and isn't sure how much longer he can be without her:

September 2, 1885
Dear Wife,
I was at Roseville to day, received your letter and was so much pleased to hear from all. I am not feeling very well since I came home to day. I have a headache, the weather is all most unendurable. It looks as though the world is on fire, no wind to speak of, hot night and day. I have got all the work I can do. The hogs are seethering all around the country. I am going up tomorrow and gather them up and sell them for what ever I can get. I think it doubtful if I can go to the Mts., would like to very much.
I think I will be obliged to move the turkeys, the

feed is getting short. So you see, I am pinched all around.

Things at our place are doing tolerably well. Am pleased to hear that all are enjoying them selves. As far as my part I cannot say that I have an over supply of enjoyment.

I think it is about as cheap to come home on the cars, by the time one takes a wagon and pay all expenses. They are about as much, besides taking the hot sun and dust.

I do not know how much longer you can stay but I do not think I can indulge you a great while longer.

*Love to all and kiss the children for me
Husband W. F. Fiddyment*

(They have three children at this point; Ira, Frank, and now Mabel, six months.)

A few years later another correspondence from Walter to Ella in the spring of 1891 has a different tone altogether. This time Ella is visiting her family at their home near Auburn. It is springtime, a season that is much more agreeable to Walter. Spring fever may have taken hold of Walter as he is very much missing Ella. Sons Ira and Frank, now ages 10 and 9, are working with him on the ranch. They have a housekeeper who does the laundry and cooking. Walter is quite impressed with Ella's brother, George, at having set 31 turkey eggs:

*Roseville March 30 1891
My Dear and Beloved Wife Ella
Your welcome letter was received Saturday and read with a great deal of satisfaction. I am exceedingly pleased to hear that you are enjoying yourself so much and hope you will take in all the sights. Drink the dew of the blooming flowers and*

revel in the beauties of nature. I know among the hills is the place for one to feast the eyes on the beauties of nature. Enjoye it.

The boys are well, also my self. And my dear teacher is enjoying her self. And last but not least the fair manipulator of the culinary prossess is well and has our meals on time. She has washed once and will wash again tomorrow. Every thing is carried on in tip top order.

Separated the nearby sheep today will commence to shear tomorrow. I also go to Sac city tomorrow, and Mrs. George Bond will accompany me. Some time the wind blows from the north and then again from the south and occasionally we have a lull. The air is freighted with the fragrance of spring. Oh! The loveliest time of all the year, on every hand nature is putting forth all of its strength. Bill is well and tending closely to his turkeys - have several set. Mrs. George Bond took supper with us tonight. Mr. Bond has thirty-one turkeys set. How is that, hope he will have good luck.

My Darling little pet if I could only draw you to my bosome tonight. Does Mabel and Russell speak of their father?

*From your Husband
W.F. Fiddyment*

(The couple have four children now with one on the way. Ira is 10, Frank is 9, Mabel is 6 and Russell five. Ella is six-months pregnant with Marjorie.)

In a return letter to Walter the next month, Ella is full of news. She expresses great concern about her mother (who has la grippe; a bad case of the flu) and also assures her husband she is staying productive. The mention of Aunt Margery's passing is referring to Walter's mother's sister. The eggs they will set are turkey

Walter Fiddyment, center, poses with members of the family. An elderly Elizabeth Jane is seated in the buggy to the right, circa 1905.

eggs, confirming that the Fiddyments were in the turkey business starting in Walter's generation. Ella mentions her father [Augustus Bond, master brick mason] keeping busy working his trade. This is a couple who obviously care a great deal for each other:

Auburn April 3rd, 1891
Dear Walter,
You could not have been more pleased to receive my letter than I was to hear from you and all. I hope the boys are doing well. Mama thinks of them a great deal, as well as their dear papa. It was sad to read the notice of dear Aunt Margery's death. We are all alarmed about mother to day and night. If she is not better tomorrow morning we will have the Doctor. The children say they are lonesome to see papa and the boys but we like to stay here.

Sunday April 5th
Mother is real sick to day it may be the effects of the medicine, but she thinks it is la grippe. Pa thinks about Tuesday he will take us home. It is

time for me to be moving but I would like to see ma feeling better before I go.
Pa has been working the most of the time since I've been here at his trade. I am going to bring down some choice eggs to set when I come that Effie has been saving for me, she wants me to have them rather than to sell them, because they are from such good stock. Tell Ira and Frankie that mamma is going to bring down some strawberry plants and they are blooming now. They can fix a nice place to plant them where they can get water and they can have them for their own.
It is not like I am losing time altogether. I am doing necessary sewing when I am well, or am not riding. They are pleased that George is having so many turkeys set so early. Pa got some medicine from the doctor for ma.
Love for yourself and Ira and Frankie
Lovingly your wife
Ella

Their children write to their grandparents. In just a few lines this young child sums up life on the ranch. Sibling Florence is about two-years old:

Feb 18 1899
Dear Grandma,
"Papa put some pigs in the barn yard and Florence is afraid to go out of the yard. We got the first turkey egg yesterday. We have 40 turkey hens and we have a pony named Mack and if two get on him he will buck."
From your loving grandchild

Their lives were busy, but even so, the couple ensured they did their part within the local community. Roseville was little more than a whistle stop but the Fiddyments were supportive and wanted to be part of the town that was starting to build. Walter and Ella were active in the local Presbyterian Church and an agrarian movement called the Grangers.* Walter also became a member of the Odd Fellows in February of 1883.

When the 19th century came to an end Roseville looked somewhat similar to the way it was in the 1870's. The area never had the chance to grow much beyond a train stop for farmers and ranchers. The population at the turn of the century consisted mostly of friends and neighbors and had remained steady at about 250 residents.

But in a few short years many changes would take place. Roseville was on the brink of a period of enormous growth, and Walter's mother would not live to see it. ❧

*Grangers were an agricultural organization created to promote ranching and farming pursuits in the latter half of the 19th century.

14

Death of Elizabeth Jane

Elizabeth Jane's fate had been a lifetime of great challenges. The hurdles she faced seemed impossible, but she was successful because she remained persistent and faithful in every step of her journey. Her community adored her and her children deeply loved and respected her.

She was a two-time widow who raised five children to adulthood mostly on her own. For their livelihood she ran hundreds of acres of ranchland and bought and sold thousands of acres of property. She raised her children with stern discipline but at the same time taught them to be fair and to live with a kind heart. Even with the concerns of her family and ranch, she always found time to help in the nearby community.

Everyone knew her as a kind and generous Christian woman, as well as one of the best business minds in the area. Early on she saw the potential of Roseville and invested. Atkinson tract in Roseville Heights was her land and when the time was right, it was sold for development. Atkinson Road was named in her honor. She had a barn built that stood by the railroad at the end of Pacific Street; for years the "Red Barn" was a well-known landmark in town.

But all of the busyness that was her life ended suddenly in the fall of 1905. A paralytic stroke came upon her while she was visiting her daughter. She stayed with her daughter and son-in-law, Martha and Dr. Norman Finney, in Lincoln to recover. By the next spring it seemed that she was on her way to recovery and moved back to Roseville.

At this time Roseville was transforming itself to accommodate the main railroad station that was being moved in from Rocklin. It was an exciting time and Elizabeth Jane was surely relishing in the activity. Her tenacity and spirit seemed to overcome her ailments and this made her family and friends hopeful. They all knew this woman, and they knew that there was very little that could keep Elizabeth Jane down.

Hers had been a long and arduous life and the effects of the stroke eventually overcame her. Even with the doctor's valiant efforts and the family's prayers, she was not able to rally. With her children and grandchildren gathered around giving her comfort, Elizabeth Jane peacefully passed away at 3:00 in the afternoon on June 19, 1906.

Saying goodbye was a sad occasion for all. Funeral services were held at the Presbyterian Church, and the procession to the cemetery was the largest in Roseville history.

She had been named one of the three largest individual taxpayers in the county and upon her death her estate was worth a small fortune. Her property was willed to her children. Saying goodbye to this incredible pioneer was akin to saying goodbye to an era. ༀ

This photo of Elizabeth Jane was likely taken in the early 1900's.

DEATH OF MRS. E. J. ATKINSON

Pioneer Woman Who Had Lived in this County for Almost Half a Century Is No More.

Peacefully and calm, like unto a child falling to sleep upon its mother's breast, Mrs. E. J. Atkinson, who has been in enfeebled health for many months past, breathed her last Tuesday afternoon at 3 o'clock, surrounded by loved ones who did all that human power was capable of doing to stay the grim reaper.

Last fall while Mrs. Atkinson was visiting in Lincoln at the home of her daughter, Mrs. Dr. W. N. Finney, she suffered a paralytic stroke, from which she never recovered and which was the cause of her death. Although at times she seemed to be on the road to recovery and those who knew and loved her for her gentle disposition and kindness of heart were inspired with the hope that she would be spared, the weight of time and burden of many years of faithful endeavor had left their impress upon the once strong constitution and the decree that comes to all things earthly was inexorable.

Early in the spring when she seemed to be much improved, and at her earnest request to be once more amid the scenes of her earlier and busy life, she was brought home from Lincoln and has since that time been tenderly cared for at the home of her daughter, Mrs. R. E. L. Leavell, where she died.

15

Walter's Son, Russell, Carrying on the Family Tradition

Russell was nearly 19-years old when his grandmother died. Losing her was a sudden and sad shock to everyone, but it was especially difficult for Russell and his father. Elizabeth Jane had been the family's matriarch for more time than Russell could remember and he and his father had often sought her sage advice. To Russell, Elizabeth Jane was a strong, loving, and larger-than-life grandmother who always had insight he needed for both business and family matters. He was going to miss her a great deal.

Unfortunately there wasn't much time for grieving as the ranch was getting larger and more demanding. Russell, and his brothers Ira and Frank, continued their ranching efforts while their father oversaw their activities.

Elizabeth Jane's will was executed and in the course of a year's time her property was divided among her four living children, Walter, Martha, John and Georgia. With a business mind like his mother, Walter invested. In 1910 he went into business with G. Lohse, establishing the Fiddyment & Lohse grocery store on Vernon

Street near the present day Washington Street underpass. After a prosperous year the store was moved to a larger building at the corner of Vernon and Lincoln streets, and Lohse was bought out. Russell continued running the ranch while Walter engaged his son Frank to run the business and the popular location was affectionately dubbed "Fiddyment Block."

With both the store and ranch running well, the family enjoyed prosperous times. The primary

ROSEVILLE PRESS-TRIBUNE

"At the new location the store prospered and for many years was the leading mercantile establishment in this vicinity, expanding from a grocery store into a dry goods and general store."

Russell Frederick Fiddyment,
circa 1891.

source of income on the ranch came from raising sheep, and to a lesser degree, turkeys and hogs. Russell was the only one of Walter's three sons to continue working the family's original ranch land. He was used to the hard work, having learned alongside his father all of his life. He was the main manager of the operation, but his father gave a hand whenever he could.

Russell's mother, Ella Fiddyment, writes to her daughter Mabel in November of 1914:

"Papa wrote about being out to the farm and help-ing Russell to load hogs early in the morning."

In the same letter Ella reminisces about one particularly funny time that she recalled Russell and Walter working together:

"It made me think of the early morning starts they used to take for one trip or another, to haul grains or hay or drive stock somewhere. [There was] a load of cowhides and sheep pelts that was the most outland-ish load I have any remembrance of. It beats any imaginary view ever thought of to see it bobbing and dangling till the team went out of sight. [It] is enough to make me laugh at the very thought of it. It were ugly but they brought forth the value in money."

For the next many years Russell worked the ranch while his father and brother Frank worked the store in Roseville. In the early 1920's Roseville also continued to grow and Vernon Street, where the Fiddyment Block was located, experienced a nice revival. Newer, more substantial structures were replacing older buildings. Where there wasn't new construction there was remodeling going on. The little town was benefitting from the heady prosperous days of the 1920's.

At this time Russell's parents, Walter and Ella moved out of the ranch house and into town. Grove Street was part of a new and developing neighborhood with Vernon Street and the cen-ter of town a short walk away. Their new home was situated perfectly next to the flourishing town's activities.

Spring planting in the early days on the Fiddyment ranch.

In April of 1923 George Haman writes to his brother-in-law Ira Fiddyment and talks about Roseville and Vernon Street:

"There are several new buildings in Roseville since you was here. You won't know the place when you see it. Vernon St. seems to be taking the lead."

It was a busy time and Russell had his fair share of work, but he wasn't so busy that he didn't catch the eye of a certain young lady. A friend of his, Carl Sawtelle, introduced the alluring Miss Cora Spangler and it wasn't long before the two knew they had something special. Maybe it was the turkey he provided for Cora and her girlfriends for Thanksgiving. She was very happy to have it, and she and the girls invited Russell to join in the feast. It was a good match! The couple joined in Holy Matrimony on April 5, 1920. At that time, Russell moved off the ranch and into town with his bride. They resided on S. Lincoln Street, not far from Russell's parents. It was about a seven-mile commute to the ranch but the newly married man of the house happily obliged.

Prosperity in the 1920's brought all of the family into town and beyond. A home was purchased in Berkeley for the elder Fiddyments, Ella and Walter, as a second home. Russell built a summer home in the mountains at a long-time favorite family camping spot for their summer getaways. Activities on the ranch continued to expand and a new lambing barn was built in 1923 alongside a recently built harvester barn. But with all the family members busy and living in town, the old ranch house was vacant.

George Haman is concerned about the situation and writes to Ira Fiddyment:

"The ranch house is empty. Fences fall down, house decaying, desolation on all sides. Nobody in the big house at all." – April 16, 1923

The 40-year-old homestead stood empty. All around it sheep were grazing, grain was being grown, and turkeys were being raised. But with no one to tend to its care, Mother Nature was working quickly to reclaim the house. With the family not ready or willing to sell, it was decided that a caretaker would live in the residence so at least some preservation of the property could be realized.

Continuing to expand his business, in 1924 Walter made a deal to replace the structure at Fiddyment block (corner of Vernon and Lincoln Streets) with a new building. In a letter to her son Ira, Ella describes the activity:

"Father is having a big brick store building made and it is to be divided up into more than one store. The store on the corner of Lincoln and Vernon is to be changed. The Roseville National Bank is to occupy the corner and the rest of it is to be divided into 3 small stores. They expect to move all the dry goods out of the store into the new store, they expect to start moving next Sat. night. It will be a busy time for several days but it is all planned out so I suppose things will move like clockwork."

To Ira from his sister Florence, also describing the new building:

"Did mother tell you about all the buildings that have gone up in Roseville this year? Well you wouldn't know the town! Dad has built a new store on Vernon Street and is remodeling the building where it used to be; the Roseville National

Bank is going in there when it is finished. New buildings, old ones burned, or were torn down."

Rent and proceeds from Fiddyment Block, along with proceeds from the ranch, helped to further secure the financial stability of the family in the 1920's.

Ella is thrilled with her family's success and is enjoying a visit from her grandson, she writes:

"Russell called in this afternoon and brought Russell Frederick in, he said he wanted to come and see his grandmother Fiddyment before going out to the ranch to feed the sheep. Russell said they are about through lambing, they have over 3500 lambs. It has been wonderful weather for lambing season." – Feb 12, 1924, To son Ira

A year later Ella is still keeping track of her son's success, and writes about Russell's surprisingly successful turkey operation:

"Russell made lots of money on turkeys this year. He bought and raised 3500 turkeys, more money than on his sheep. He fed them on the rice fields in Sutter Basin and shipped them from there for .41 cents per pound at the shipping point at the place where they dressed them. There were about 1000 gobblers. It is hard work getting them off but

he was lucky to get them shipped before the heavy rain. He had good help ..." To son Ira, Feb 11, 1925

By the spring of 1925 the turkey business is proving to be so successful that Russell's brother, Frank, has decided to give it a try on his nearby ranchland. Walter agrees and hires a new manager for the store, which frees up Frank to run his new turkey venture. Mother (Ella) shares the news with son Ira while offering some sage advice:

"Frank is going to try and raise turkeys. Getting the turkeys off on the river where there is plenty of green grass and hoppers and crickets and water is where the secret lies."

The attempt is a success! Brothers Russell and Frank have become good business partners and on November 14, 1925, Ella writes to Ira bragging a bit about his siblings:

"Frank and Russell are engaged in turkey raising. They have more than 5000 and are counting on .40 cents a pound and more."

For the next several years, Ella continues to share the good news of the brothers' newfound success. No doubt she hopes her son Ira will come home from living in southern California and perhaps join in the profitable family business.

"Russ is doing fine and has a nice new Willis Knight Car now, it certainly is a beauty." – June 4, 1925

"Russell and Frank expect to dress about 2,000 turkeys for Christmas." – Dec 13, 1925

The roaring 20's continue on, and the Fiddyment family are happy and grateful for their success. At a family birthday party and picnic visit to the ranch in March of 1926, Ella describes with delight how turkeys and lambs fill the scene:

"Frank and Russell have 650 turkeys to raise. The man was feeding them out by the wool house tonight when we left, they were a sight, great big red headed bronze stock, they are just starting to lay."

"Russell has a lot of ewes and lambs running in the field south of the house and in the east field, they are looking fine."

Russell and Cora were certainly keeping busy, both at the ranch and at home. By spring of 1927 the young couple had four children; three boys (Russell Frederick age 6, David age 4, John age 2) and a new baby girl (Coralie). It was evident they had outgrown their little house on South Lincoln Street.

The logical choice for a larger family home was the old ranch house. It was decided they would move and while they didn't intend to stay in the home permanently, it would accommodate their needs in the interim. Repairs and restorations were completed, along with fresh new wallpaper and paint. The finishing touch was the hiring of a fumigator to ensure all traces of Mother Nature were eradicated.

Continuing to share the family's news, Ella writes to son Ira:

"We went out to the ranch yesterday… Russell had the yard all plowed up and dug up and a clover sown along part of it, and a garden in part of it.

The old place looks real nice but they are not going to live there, only until they build a new house.

Russell has two bands of sheep on his rented summer range, above Colfax and they feed along until they get up near Emigrant Gap and by that time they will be able to go on to French Meadows. The two ranges go together. He ought to do well if his herders have good luck. Father rode down to the Sac River with Russell today, he says they have a fine crop of barley this year but Russell is racing day and night and can hardly take time to eat and sleep."
– May 14, 1928

A little later on in the year, Ella is pleased that her grandchildren want to see her before starting work at the ranch. She writes:

"He [Russell] was here today with his 3 little boys, the oldest Russell Jr. is in his second year of school and has dinner with us every school day. Mabel is his teacher. David and Johnnie are rugged little fellows. Little Coralie is strong and healthy walks and talks." – Oct 17, 1928 Ella to Ira

It was a prosperous time and they worked hard. On those occasions when they could take a break from working the family would get together. They very much enjoyed pleasant times with one another.

In two letters in 1929, August and November, Ella writes to Ira:

"Russell has his sheep to pasture this summer in Utah on the other side of Salt Lake. He went with Frank to sell them, they took turns driving the Buic, camped on the side of the road and stayed in some fine hotels also. They crossed the desert in the night. Lambs were fat. They were sold and shipped on to Chicago." – August 18, 1929

"Father and I went out and staid all night at the ranch with the children while Cora and Russell went to a card party. Yesterday we went back and had a turkey dinner with them, every thing was very nice. It looks very nice out at the ranch. The old fire place throws out the warmth as freely as it used to and as cheerily. Imagine us sitting round it yesterday. Florence played on Cora's piano a good many numbers and all enjoyed hearing her play. We have a telephone out to the ranch now." – November 19, 1929

The ranch house was proving to be a convenient home for them, so Russell and Cora had decided to continue to live there a little while longer. Their plan was to build a new house in another year or so. But just as often as we plan our future, life will have a different plan altogether. At this time the world was about to change. For the Fiddyment family, the 1929 stock market and subsequent Great Depression not only altered their plans, it nearly created their demise. ❧

Russell Fiddyment & Cora Spangler m. 1920
Russell Jr.
David
John
Coralie

16

Roseville and The Great Depression

Americans were fully unprepared for Black Thursday, October 24, 1929. The stock market crash and subsequent run on banks created nationwide panic. No person or city escaped financial burden in the Great Depression, and Roseville certainly felt its share of the disaster.

In 1930 the city's leading employer, the Southern Pacific Railroad, decreased its work force and put over 230 workers out of jobs. A year later the remaining employees felt a stinging 10 percent pay cut. Businesses were closing their doors, and for the first time in a decade, Vernon Street had empty buildings.

In an effort to help, in January of 1931 the City Council appropriated $1,000 to be used for jobless relief, and by March some 30 families received regular assistance. But the numbers of the needy continued to grow. During the winter of 1930-31 $1,500 in cash was raised to help take care of over 100 families, but even that was a shortfall as it was reported that over 200 families in the area were now in serious trouble.

The town rallied with organizations and individuals banning together to donate food, clothing and money. In a few short months a charity store was opened downtown to help distribute donations.

After two years of rising unemployment and no relief in sight, the nation had grown weary of its leadership. The people of Roseville agreed, and in November of 1932 local voters overwhelmingly elected Franklin Delano Roosevelt as President. Within a year of his inauguration aid to the country began in earnest.

With the help of grant money the city of Roseville put people to work paving miles of city streets, along with building curbs, gutters and storm sewers. In 1934, despite the now full-blown depression, municipal improvements continued to be made. The city took over the garbage system and provided service for its citizens at only 50 cents a month. Then the city used more federal money to buy out the antiquated local water company and funded a program to build new water pipes, repairs and upgrades.

Recognizing that its citizens were still dealing with economic challenges, in 1936 an already low city tax rate of $1.75 was reduced to 75 cents per $100 assessed valuation. The same tax rate was in place until the 1948 post-war building boom.

But the nation was at a crawl, and it continued to be a difficult time for everyone. In an effort to escape the gloom and doom Roseville's citizens found ways to have fun.

Movies were a popular pastime and the Roseville Theater on Vernon Street provided the venue. Southern Pacific and service clubs hosted picnics in Royer Park, often with baseball games as a popular main attraction.

In 1935 and 1936, the Chamber of Commerce along with the City sponsored public street fairs on Vernon. The road was blocked off and the well-attended event usually ended with a big street dance.

By the end of the 1930's the nation's economy started to show signs of turning around. Prohibition had been lifted, and after several years the new tax revenue started to make a difference. Now the nation overall began to feel that the times were starting to turn around. It had been a long, arduous decade. ❧

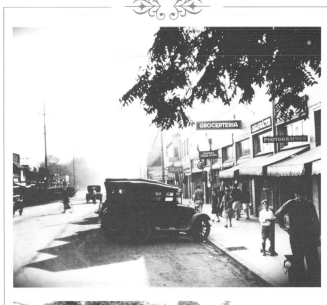

Top: Fiddyment Block, circa 1920's.

Bottom: Parade in front of Fiddyment Block, circa 1930's.

Left: Calling card for Ira Fiddyment.

17

The Fiddyment Family and the Great Depression

As if it were foreshadowing the challenging years to come, in January 1930 a rare snowstorm struck Roseville and the surrounding area. As she watches the snow fall outside, Ella is growing concerned and expresses some of her worry as she writes to her son Ira:

"Carl told us that a regular blizzard is going on in the mountains tonight. He saw an engine and snow plow starting to the mountains to help clear the track of snow up there. We are having a stormy night here and father says it will be bad for the young lambs. The big creek has been bank full before this last storm, so now it must be high."

It is evident that economic times are already affecting the family. Russell's finances are strained, and he is feeling overwhelmed with responsibilities on the ranch. It is starting to take a toll on his health. In another letter during the same month Ella writes about his situation:

"Russell is not well he has spells of faintness. Now he is worried about the lambs and the price

of turkeys and at this time short of money and at this severe season and all it helps make him nervous."
– Ella to Ira, January 10, 1930

The family's main income was from raising sheep as it provided two annual periods of good revenue: wool in the springtime from shearing the ewes (mother sheep) and later on in the season the lamb crop that was sold to butcher.

It was a normal practice for Russell to borrow money against the sheep every year to pay expenses, then when income was produced, he would pay off the loan. In the early years of the 1930's wool, veal and mutton started to lose their value on the market, but Russell adjusted his efforts and continued his usual loan cycle with Bank of America. But in 1933 prices suddenly plummeted. For the first time ever the value of the bank loan became greater than the value of the sheep. When this happened the manager of the bank requested a meeting with Russell.

Snow on the (once again remodeled) Fiddyment ranch house.

The Fiddyment family had been conducting business with Bank of America for years and had an excellent relationship with the manager. Russell fully expected they would work with him through the slow period. Unfortunately that was not to be the case. The hard-working rancher never suspected what was about to happen.

The bank manager explained that he had no choice but to call the loan. Russell argued that the value of the sheep would certainly go back up and that his track record of repaying his debts was impeccable. He stated that he was confident the upcoming seasonal shearing and subsequent sale of wool would more than cover his loan. He implored the bank manager to give him more time.

But no amount of discussion would change the manager's mind. Giving no regard to their past relationship or Russell's payment history, the full amount of the loan became due and payable immediately. This left Russell with no choice but to sell. The thousands of sheep that were his family's main source of livelihood were sold at auction at a huge discount. The money made on the sale did not come close to covering the value of the loan, and Russell was forced into loan default.

It was a sudden and devastating blow. He still had the turkey operation, but it wasn't nearly enough to sustain the family. He had four children and a wife, with hundreds of acres of ranchland and a house to maintain. He immediately started searching for opportunities, but money was scarce and he quickly realized he was on the brink of financial disaster.

Adding to the despair, on November 1, 1933 Russell's ailing father passed away. Walter Fiddyment had been a wonderful patriarch. He was a loving father and grandfather who insisted that his family maintain strong moral values and that his businesses be run with integrity. But the onset of the Great Depression years took its toll and despite all of his efforts, his business dealings had suffered in the end.

Upon his death the family's wealth was tallied, and what investment income there was had to be utilized to support Russell's mother Ella, his sister Florence, and to a lesser degree, his brother Ira. At a time when it was sorely needed, there was no money for Russell and his family. While he mourned the loss of his father, he was also hugely concerned with keeping his family out of economic ruin.

Turkey farming became the mainstay for the Fiddyment family during the Great Depression.

Turkeys

Springtime is about new beginnings and so it was for Russell Fiddyment in the spring of 1934. He had been ramping up his turkey business in an effort to offset the loss of his sheep, but he could only provide what the demand would bear. He could increase production, but the local turkey market was maxed out. However, there was another part of the world that not only demanded more poultry, they wanted Fiddyment poultry.

In the spring of 1934 Russell received a phone call from the head of a wholesale house in San Francisco telling him that the demand for Fiddyment turkeys had just become enormous. Russell had sold to the wholesale house for years and through those sales some of his turkeys had been sold to Australia. When the ships from Australia came back for another load in San Francisco their request was specifically for Fiddyment turkeys. He now had a huge demand for turkeys! It was the opportunity he needed, but he was financially strapped and had no ready resources to expand to meet this great demand so quickly. But that didn't matter, he

was a Fiddyment and he had made up his mind to go after the business, even though he had no idea how he was going to do it.

He explored many avenues with all resulting in dead-ends. It was the Great Depression and money was nowhere to be found. In a last attempt he did something he thought he might never do again, he sought help from a bank. Cora Fiddyment, Russell's wife tells the story best during a living history interview:

"One day Russ was in the bank and George Zoller was the head of the Capitol National, he was president and he saw Russ down on the floor and he came down and was talking to him and he said, 'Russ, do you need any money?' Russ said, 'I guess I need it more than I need anything else.' And Mr. Zoller said, 'How much do you need?' And Russ told him and he said, 'It's right here for you.'"

It was an incredible moment. David Fiddyment, (Russell's son), shares some insight about the situation, also during a living history interview:

"It was certainly gratifying to think that a man had that much confidence in my dad's ability. It started a whole new relationship with that bank, and more particular George Zollar. He was Pa's banker for the turkey business and [eventually] the sheep business [again]."

The money was loaned, and Russell was able to increase his turkey crop tenfold. Capitol National Bank, and especially George Zoller, saved Russell from financial ruin and got him started in a business that would sustain the Fiddyment family for many years.

The adversity felt in the 1930's was a grueling time for the entire family; especially for Russell and Cora. They only knew they would just keep trying and do the best they could. The plans for a new house were scrapped, but it seemed to be okay. They had been through the most difficult time of their lives but instead of lamenting their losses, they came to the conclusion that family and good friends were more important than living in a new house. The ranch house was their family's home and that was where they were going to stay.

Russell survived the depression years and ended up with a strong business in raising turkeys. The failing economy was being revived. Now Russell and Cora could focus on raising their part of the fourth generation of the Fiddyment family. ✎

A 1932 sales receipt showing a major source of the family's income.

18

Death of Walter Fiddyment

Walter had been ailing for about a year. His diagnosis from the doctor was an inflammation of his nervous system. The doctor said there really wasn't anything to be done except to keep him as comfortable as possible. His final weeks brought a lot of pain but then, on the first day in November of 1933, Walter breathed his last and was in pain no more.

He was born to a strong, enterprising mother and he followed in her strength. When she was widowed a second time, Walter, at only 11 years old, stood by her side and took on the male responsibilities of their livelihood. He grew up working among the stately oaks, tall grasses and wild roses in the land that was west of the tiny town of Roseville. Springtime was his favorite season. When the oaks leafed out, and the streams were flowing, and the flowers were in full color and fragrant bloom, he was happiest.

He married Ella Bond in 1879 and at that time settled into the 80 acres next to his mother's property. With the help of his father-in-law, he turned the small cabin residing there into a proper home. His land holdings grew and so did his family. He and Ella raised six children on his ranch: Ira, Frank, Mabel, Russell, Marjorie, and Florence.

His family was the center of his world. He took his boys with him to work on the ranch from the time they could walk, and he treated his daughters with care and respect, encouraging them to become their own person and to get an education.

He was a devout Christian man and had been chosen as an elder in the Roseville Presbyterian Church in 1901. At his memorial service the organ that he donated was played and in his honor a blue cypress tree was planted on the church grounds.

Walter saw enormous changes in his life. As a young boy he saw the first locomotive running in California. He worked a plow from the back of a horse as a young man, and then managed whole teams of horses with more sophisticated plows on his own family's ranch. He saw Roseville grow from a railroad shipping point to an actual town. Inventions as simple as barbwire, and complex as the telegraph and radio, were part of his life. But the automobile was an invention that took him some getting used to.

His grandson David Fiddyment tells the story of his grandfather Walter's first car:

"My granddad had a horse and buggy, then he started using a car. He went to town one time, it was early 1900's and he purchased an automobile, and he came to the gate out there when he came to the ranch. He didn't know how to use the brakes so when he got up to the gate and the car kept going he shouted "whoa you" "whoa you! Damn you! Whoa!" And he went and drove right through the gate!"

He never stopped working. At the age of 60, when his boys took over the ranch duties, he began a retail business. Up until the Great Depression he bought and sold real estate, was a landlord to many businesses, and was always on hand to help his boys, especially his son Russell on the ranch. It was all second nature to him and just the way life worked.

David Fiddyment further describes his grandfather:
"My grandfather Walter had the same strong original ideas that his predecessors had. They were pioneers. He had the pioneering spirit and understood the process of survival. The smokehouse, the hog scalding bath, all those things were part of the way of life they had to have. There was no local grocery store, they did it all themselves. Everybody that ventured into the unknown had to have that or they didn't survive."

Walter Fiddyment rests next to his mother Elizabeth Jane Crawford Fiddyment Hill Atkinson, at the Fiddyment/Hill family plot in the old Roseville Cemetery.

PIONEER PASSES

— Cut Courtesy Sacramento Bee.
W. F. Fiddyment, Roseville pioneer citizen, who passed away in Berkeley Wednesday evening, following a lingering illness.

W. F. FIDDYMENT SUCCUMBS AFTER LENGTHY ILLNESS

W. F. Fiddyment, one of Roseville's oldest and best known residents, passed away Wednesday night in Berkeley following an illness of a year's duration. The deceased lacked but two days of being 83 years of age, his birthday being today.

Fiddyment came to Roseville with his mother from Illinois, where he was born on November 3, 1850. He was two years of age when he made the crossing to Roseville across the Isthmus of Panama. He settled on the Fiddyment ranch just west of the city and has made his home here since that time. When the deceased first settled here, the present site of Rose-

19

Russell's son, David Everett Fiddyment, The Fourth Generation

Russell and Cora entered the era of the Great Depression with four young children in tow. Their second son, David, was born in 1923. The family was living in town at their South Lincoln Street home when his mother Cora made this diary entry:

"He came April 20th, Friday at 2:45 p.m. at the Alta Bates Hospital (Berkeley). Russell came at one p.m. having driven from Roseville in 4 hours and in a short while our babe came. We called him David and he weighed 7lbs 15oz and is a perfectly normal child. Little Russell loves his baby brother and says 'Mother isn't he cute, see his little feets.'" – from the diary of Cora Fiddyment

David was born into The Roaring '20's. The economy was booming, jobs were plentiful, and great minds were at work on new technology. What life looked like on the streets was even changing. One of David's earliest memories was of the newest mode of transportation, the automobile. He recalls:

"When I was a youngster the automobile had shown up on the scene. It had probably been around for 15 or 20 years and it evolved very rapidly and the horses went away very rapidly. The Model T was a pollution fighter! The pollution was horse manure! It was quite the thing at the time."

Mass production and Henry Ford had made it possible for anyone to buy a car. For about $300, and as long as you could see over the hood, both a car and driver's license could be had. But people didn't usually get rid of their horses. In those early years horses were still the most practical method of getting around, and it was common to see people with both modes of transport side by side. David muses about those early roads and their tricky navigation:

"... there were no paved roads. They were basically wagon roads and in the wintertime they were nothing more than muddy ruts. You'd get

David Everett Fiddyment, b. 1923

stuck in the mud, often. There were times when the only way to get out was to get a team of horses from a neighbor and you would hook up to the front of the car and it would pull you out. In the summertime the loose dirt on the surface of the road would kind of realign itself and it became wash boarding. I remember vividly the cars would rattle and it was very noisy. You could only go about 10 miles an hour without shaking the car apart! Every once in a while the county would come along with a grader and smooth the washboards out then it was not too long before they were back again."

Another popular mode of transport was the train. It had been around much longer than the car and of course Roseville was quite prevalent as a train station. Little boys can be especially fascinated with the giant locomotives, and David was no exception. His older brother had a train set and he wanted one too! He recalls with a smile:

"I was so small but I remember sitting in Santa's lap and telling him very sincerely what I wanted for Christmas. I don't know if my mom was standing by or not but I firmly stated to Santa that I wanted an electric train for Christmas. Well, Christmas came and I didn't get a train. One day after Christmas there was a knock at the door and the postal deliveryman came with a package from Weinstocks. I was sure that package was my electric train. It wasn't. Now I was upset."

The train obsession stayed with him.

"I remember a year or two after that disappointing Christmas we were visiting Grandma. It was Christmas time again and much of the family was visiting. In those days they went by the motto that 'kids are to be seen and not heard.' It happened that my aunt had decided to decorate the big table and included a little electric train. I thought sure that was my train! I was so excited!

"But it wasn't my train and I guess I made kind of a fuss about it and started crying. I think I was being rude and in those days it was rude to make a fuss about an issue, especially if you were a young child."

David doesn't elaborate but it was highly likely that he got into a little trouble over making such a fuss. He finally did get a train but it wasn't until many years later and a certain Christmas that involved another little boy.

Living on South Lincoln Street

Young boys are wonderful adventurers. While they play with their trains and toy trucks their imaginations can take them to places where they will spend hours. Perfect for this activity was Royer Park and it was within walking distance of the South Lincoln Fiddyment house.

In those days the park was also a small zoo that included a bear and monkeys as well as peacocks and lots of ducks roaming around. The monkeys were David's favorite. The Fiddyment boys were often spotted playing among the trees and playground equipment. A little later on, David attended Boy Scout meetings there at the Veteran's Memorial Hall.

He would also join his brothers and father on errands at the ranch, leaving his mother to tend to the house. Cora, who was very pregnant at the time, writes about one of those days:

"I am all alone today. Russ has taken the three boys with him to the ranch and on to Wheatland. Bessie the girl has gone out. These last few days have been very trying, waiting for the arrival of our fourth child and this time we are hoping for a girl. I am expecting its arrival most any time now. It is moving and turning around a great deal lately."
– Cora Fiddyment diary, March 10, 1927

In 1927 Russell Fiddyment moved his family from in-town Roseville out to the family ranch house. By this time the house had been remodeled several times, including the remodel that Russell completed. The house is pictured on the right. On the left is David Fiddyment at about 8-years old.

Cars getting stuck in the mud was a common occurrence.

A few days later she writes:

"Coralie Fay Fiddyment arrived March 14, Monday at 4:45 pm at Mater Misericordiae Hospital, Sacramento (now Mercy Hospital). We are overjoyed at the arrival of our girl."

Having grown to be a family of six, the family found their South Lincoln Street home a little too crowded. A few months after the birth of their baby girl, the Russell Fiddyment family— which now included mother Cora, children Russell Jr., John, David and baby Coralie— moved. They would be in the country now, seven miles out of town living in the old Fiddyment ranch home. It was spring of 1927.

Living in the Ranch House

One of David's favorite early memories of the ranch house was the upstairs bathroom and specifically the bathtub. He shares:

"It was just enormous, it felt like you could swim in it. It was about six feet long and as youngsters we would have a grand time playing in it."

In those days a wood stove was used to heat the water and cold baths were as frequent as hot ones.

A year or two after they had moved onto the ranch, David's mother Cora recalls a bit of a disaster involving baby turkeys. His father Russell had been in the turkey business for years, but he was just beginning to raise the birds from the time they hatched. Cora tells the story:

"In the west field on that little knoll up there, Russ had five little coops. You know, the A-shaped coops. And the turkeys in the coops had sat on their eggs and hatched them. Each turkey had their own little house and there were little baby turkeys just about three-weeks old.

"One Sunday Russ was busy and he asked, 'Would you go up and see if the turkeys are all right?' There was no herders for them at that time, nobody watching after them.

"So the cook and I went up to see about the turkeys, and you know, a coyote had gotten in, killed every turkey. There was nothing but

little legs of the little turkeys left and every turkey finished. The whole gang, the whole business was wiped out. Next time he took more care of them."

It was a lesson learned about coyotes, especially with baby turkeys around.

Russell was raising turkeys but still earning the bulk of his livelihood from the sheep business. Then, at the beginning of the Depression era, David at age 8 was fully aware of the incident involving his father's loan recall and his parents' concern. While his dad was forced to sell all their sheep, he doesn't remember any particular hardships.

But he does remember that they made the best of it. Some of their most memorable times were when the family worked together. David remembers a scene from his past that involved his mom and canning peaches.

He tells the story:

"I remember as a youngster dad came home with five lug boxes of peaches. Mom knew they were coming. She told her two sisters to come on out, 'We're going to can peaches!' Canning was a day's work. You would make a lye solution out of hot water, put the peaches in, take the outer peeling off. They were canned as peach halves in a quart jar and stored in the cooler. We needed to prepare each year for winter and the seasons."

And prepare they did. As the women worked in the kitchen the men worked in the fields. David knew the ranch hands schedule by heart.

"The men would get up at 4:00 a.m. and would water the horses. Then they would have breakfast at 5:30 a.m. After breakfast they would harness the horses and prepare them for a day of work. On a three-horse team they could pull two 10-inch bottom plows. They would plow 20 inches at a time out in the fields. They worked to 10:00 a.m. then the cook would bring the chuck wagon out to feed the men. They ate again at noon, then again at 2:00 p.m. and at 6:00 p.m. they had a big meal."

David remembers as a youngster working in the fields with his dad. He recalls his father being an extremely innovative man who always figured out what needed to be done. As he shares those days of growing up on the ranch he makes mention of an important fact:

"If anything was not completed on time, or completed incorrectly, the family's very existence would be compromised. In those days there was no discussion about not doing a task, it simply had to be done. Children were put to work as soon as they were capable and teenagers simply did not have opportunity to question or opt out of family chores."

BIRTHDAY PARTY

One year David's sister, Coralie, invited the entire school class to attend her birthday party at the family's home on the ranch. One of her classmates in attendance recently told about an event that he remembered happening that day.

It was springtime, and springtime on the ranch is beautiful. At one point in the festivities the young preteens were invited to watch the turkeys being fed. The group gathered outside and as they were watching the thousands of turkeys roaming about, the feed truck came on the scene. The vehicle pulled to a stop right in the middle of the flock and one of the Fiddyment brothers climbed out of the driver's seat and onto the back of the truck.

The turkeys were well aware that this was feeding time so they immediately quieted and gathered around the vehicle. The young man stood tall, then with a loud and sudden voice he shouted out, "Are there any Republicans out there?" to which all the thousands of turkeys loudly replied "gobble, gobble, gobble."

It was a presidential election year and the young man wanted to share his thoughts. A short speech was made, and the classmates went away with a fitting lesson in turkeys and politics that day.

For this young partygoer it was one of life's indelible moments!

– Story courtesy of Kenneth Lonergan, past Superintendent of Schools for Placer County

Aerial photograph of the ranch.

20

Sheep

With the exception of a short time during the Great Depression, the Fiddyment ranch always had sheep. The sheep business had two periods that provided sources of revenue; income from the wool at shearing time, and income from selling the lamb crop when they were sold to butcher. There was a reason the family had chosen sheep versus cattle, and David explains the choice:

"You could run more sheep on an acre of ground than you could cows. Cows ate more, by the same token you were looking for pounds of meat that a band of sheep could produce versus pounds of meat that a herd of cattle could produce. There was a relationship there. Sheep liked certain feed and certain kinds of grasses, and cows could sustain themselves with lesser quality food."

The family was well-versed in the cycle of sheep raising and selling.

David explains: "Early winter was the time of year that baby lambs were born. There was very little food on the ranch, but it was a place where the herders could watch the flocks and mother sheep could have a lamb without any difficulty, normally.

"The mother sheep during that gestation period had to be in good shape so the lamb would come out in good shape. Once the lamb was born then the mother's ability to provide milk had to be considered. They had to have sustainable food on a daily basis.

"My dad in his forethought decided to build a building, and we called it the lambing barn. It was huge; it was 120 by 200 feet. You could put a whole band of sheep in the center of that building. Along the sides of the center sections he built small cribs, about four feet square, and there was a little place where they could put hay, so that one sheep could be put in there with her lamb and kept away from the rest.

"The herders would work through the center, or main block of sheep. Whenever a lamb was born the herder would pick up the lamb and the mother would follow right behind. They would put the little lamb in the crib and the mother would protect it.

"They stayed there two or three days to ensure bonding. But once in a while the mother would have twins. The herders knew just by watching the lambs whether that mother could raise

Lambing barn on the Fiddyment ranch.

them both with the amount of milk they were producing. These guys were pretty savvy.

"In most cases these herders were from Basque. There was enough demand for services for them to move to this region. These guys knew sheep herding. I think my dad relied a great deal on them.

"It took about a month or so for all the ewes to lamb out. This was about the first part of January. We were still having to feed them, but the grass was growing, it had been raining a little bit, and the temperature was beginning to climb a few degrees. There was more and more natural feed. This reduced the need for hay and

grain, which made the ranch very profitable. The weather got warmer and it grew to the point where we didn't have to feed.

"In the springtime it was just a thrill to watch baby lambs out frolicking around. They would get together and run and jump and play. It was just … it made you feel good to watch the activity going on out in the field. They grew rapidly. Long about the first of April the adult sheep had to be sheared.

"My dad, in his wisdom, built a building that he called a shearing barn. Outside that barn were fields where the main bunch of sheep were held

Walter Fiddyment, far right, looks on as three men prepare to dip sheep. Sheep dipping was performed to remove any parasites that might damage the sheep's wool.

while they were waiting to come in to be sheared. The herders would put three maybe four sheep inside the building to be sheared.

"The shearers would come in with their equipment and they would set up. The shearing equipment looked like the old dentist equipment from long ago. It had lots of arms and almost 360-degree movement. On the end they had the shearers, the clippers. One piece of equipment was a comb, on top of that was a cutter blade and it actually moved back and forth. There was a motor or generator outside that powered each station.

"Those guys would grab a sheep, put it on its back, and the sheep didn't seem to struggle. The shearers would hold their legs; they would start at the brisket and go over the top of the belly. The first cut would just open up everything, and they went along in sequence. Each cut was about three-inches wide and in about two to three minutes most of the wool was off. Then they would cut the face, then the legs. Then they would turn the sheep loose, and they would go across the alleyway into

another pen, then another herder would come in and put a brand on them.

"Our brand was a heart and it is registered with the State of California Department of Livestock. (Today this is the CDFA, California Department of Food and Agriculture.) It was an old brand, possibly from the turn of the century. There weren't many sheep growers back then.

"Then the shearer would bunch the wool together, take it off to the side, then take another sheep and continue shearing. Someone else would collect the wool together and put a paper string around it. There was two decks in the building and the upper deck was where the wool sacks were and a man on this deck would take the fleece of wool and fit it into a wool rack. A wool rack held a sack that was six feet long, six feet diameter, and 2 ½ feet across the opening. The sack fit perfectly and hung from the top.

"They would get several fleeces in the sack then a man would jump into the sack and work his legs and feet to press the wool down. He was always

Sheep grazing on land that is now part of Sun City Roseville, circa 1970's.

busy pressing wool into the sack and he was filling sacks pretty rapidly. Once the sack was full another fellow maneuvered it and sewed it up with sack twine to close it.

"The full sacks were dropped down and rolled into a pile, and they were about 200 pounds each. Two fellows would then roll and up end them where they were supposed to go."

The strength and stamina of the men doing this work had to be incredible. This part of the sheep-raising business was all hired help, but David and his brothers were required to understand it. Sometimes, amidst all the work, the boys would do as boys do and take a few moments to play. David recalls one particular afternoon when they were playing that his little sister could have gotten very hurt.

"One time as youngsters my sister Coralie wasn't very old. We were playing around the wool sacks up there, she wanted to get away from us, and she darted around the end of the pile of wool. It was the south side of the

building where there was an open door. We were up about six feet and she must not have seen the door. She just kept going not realizing she was on top of the sacks. She went flying. My dad was very disturbed, and she was crying. He brushed her off and after a while the crying stopped, and we went back to playing.

"That was just a little aside, but I remember that vividly. Coralie was the only girl in the family and she played right alongside of us, but we protected her like she was a princess!"

David goes on to finish the sheep-shearing process: *"Once the sheep were sheared the wool was stored, and there was a buyer and they would make a deal on the price. My dad knew the market. There was always buyers who were out there trying to buy for less or take advantage of somebody who didn't know what was going on, but Pa was pretty astute in his ability to negotiate with these people.*

"After the shearing was all done the sheep had a whole different look to them! I'm sure it was

a challenge for these lambs to find their mother because from the standpoint of sight and 'that's my mom over there but she didn't look the same, but her voice was the same, and oh that must be my mom!' And it wasn't long before they would get together."

Late winter and early spring are the best time for the sheep to be in the fields on the ranch. But once the weather starts to heat up the grasses quickly change and become undesirable.

"By April 20th stickers were beginning to go to seed. Stickers were what drove the sheep growers off the ranch. It was imperative because the lambs had wool on their legs and the stickers would stick in that wool. In some cases it was like a foxtail and the stickers would bore right into the skin and this hurt the ability of the sheep to hunt food. Pa was well aware of that and wanted to get them out of there before the stickers would go to seed. He was prepared for this and he had ranges all the way going up into the mountains.

"Pa had arranged with the forest service and private owners, starting around Forest Hill, to truck the sheep up and turn them out into open range. It was just wide open. No roads, no nothing, it was long before the bridge. There was always good green grass as you went up the mountain.

"The herder went up the mountain, he had a dog and a burro and he was always out there with the sheep. They would kind of fan out and feed on the grass and on the leaves off bushes. The herder would kind of mosey along and

watch the sheep, he knew where they were and they knew where he was. They would come in at night and bed down and camp. How the sheep knew to do that I never understood.

"The herder had to be aware; he always had a gun over his shoulder. Once in a while you would get a bear or a lion and the coyotes were always a risk."

Sometimes traveling in the mountains with a band of sheep posed a problem.

One particular time David recalls when the route had to be changed: *"We were down near Gold Run and there wasn't any way to get around some of the Placer mining problems that had been created. There were sheer cliffs created in places where you just couldn't move a bunch of sheep. So we had to travel along the highway! This is a continental highway, Highway 40, and we were driving a bunch of sheep right down the middle of it! The highway patrol would help us and generally they had flagmen but a bunch of sheep right in the middle of the road was quite an obstacle. The number of cars we would encounter might be three or four, which is quite a departure from where we are today. They would either let the sheep go by or they would slowly work their way through them.*

"Then we would get off the highway and back into the fields so the sheep could forage along. The herder had to pack the burro; his food, camping equipment, everything that he needed was on the back of the burro. He would put a canvas over the top of it and rope it down so the burro wouldn't lose his load. The herder

would hit him alongside the butt and he would get along and follow behind the sheep. And they kept moving.

"By mid-July when the lambs were big enough to ship they would make it to Soda Springs. At Soda Springs they had a bunch of corrals that were part of the railroad property. My dad would order a bunch of cars that would come and stop, and they would wait right there. Lambs that were sold had to go up a steep chute and into the cars.

"The lambs didn't want to go up the chute into the dark; it was something brand new to them. The dogs would jump up on the backs of the lambs, get up to their head, bite their ears, and bark in their faces. The lambs were trying to get away from the dogs so they would eventually go up the shoot. Well, once two or three would get started the rest would follow. There were usually 2,500 to 3,000 sheep to load.

"Eventually they would get the train loaded, and they would put the loaded cars back onto the main line, hook it up, and down the road they'd go.

"They would keep the rest of the sheep in the mountains until almost snow time and that could be as early as early October. Then they were brought back to the valley generally by train or truck and taken down into the district where hay was grown.

"In the fall when the hay crops were minimal, the owner of the hay fields would let the sheep people come in and forage in the fields. There were also wheat fields and sugar beets where

they had been harvested, same with cornfields; it was all good forage for the sheep. They would let the sheep people come in and get a little extra income. They would stay there until it was almost lambing time, and then they were brought back to the ranch and the cycle would start all over again." ☙

21

The Turkey Business

In the mid-to-late 1930's consumers decidedly wanted more turkey meat on their tables. This is the time period when the mechanical incubator started to be used and putting it into operation required the Fiddyments to make changes.

Every day, either the Fiddyment boys or a hired hand would carefully gather eggs from the laying turkey hens. Once they were gathered they were gently placed into a mechanical incubator. As long as there were no babies in her care the laying hens would continue to produce eggs. Once there were about 20 eggs for each laying hen, the hatched babies would be taken from the incubator and placed with a mother turkey. This was called setting.

David remembers his father setting the hens: *"I remember Pa setting, he must've set a hundred hens [each year] and each hen would hatch 20 little turkeys — that would be 2,000 babies with a hundred mothers."*

The hen and her babies would be housed in a specially designed coop and human interaction now became a key part of the process.

David recalls: *"They had a fence that would fit over the top of this coop, and once the babies were a couple weeks old they would reach in very, very quietly and grab the hen. Because she was a wild turkey she would flop her wings and if she happened to hit one of those little turkeys in there it would kill it. So they had to be very careful. But they'd grab the hen and get her out of there, and these little turkeys were in this coop and they'd scatter just like a bunch of baby quail.*

"Then the next person was to take the coop off, and the enclosure was there and you'd just have to hunt for these little turkeys. They'd just scatter, and they were under the straw and in the corners and under the grass and any place they could hide, they were there. They would take those [babies] and dad would toe mark them. He'd cut a toe off so he knew what band they belonged to. He wanted to keep them separate. Then he would put those little turkeys in a box and put them with the mother on a trailer or truck.

"Then they would go out into an open field, and they would put the coop down again and put the mother hen inside and put the babies in and she'd call the babies to her.

A ranch hand gathering eggs in the brooder house.

She would talk to them and they would respond. She would get them underneath her feathers, protect them, and care for them. The mother instinct in those birds was just unbelievable, it really was strong."

"The coop actually had two sections, the weatherproof living section and the enclosed, open-air outside section. The mother and the babies were coaxed to walk around the outside section and forage for their food. This is where the turkey herder's job came into play.

David explains: *"The herder would have a little feed and the little babies would be encouraged to eat. The mother would talk to them [the babies] and they learned. Pretty soon they kept getting bigger and bigger. At night she'd bring them in and they'd go under her feathers but as the little birdies got bigger they began to roost out on top of the rack outside."*

At this point the babies were big enough to roam about on their own and they had grown to trust the turkey herder.

David remembers: *"During the day the herder would go out in the field and they [the turkeys] would follow him. He would walk out in the fields, and they would pick up grass seed and grasshoppers and anything they could find. Little by little they would take some of the hens away, and it wasn't long, maybe three or four weeks, there would only be three or five hens in this group. Eventually it got down to where there was just a big group of baby turkeys.*

"The herder would walk out into the field and the babies would follow him. They would pick up bugs and other things so he didn't have to feed them other than back at camp."

The baby turkeys would stay on the ranch until the grasshoppers and other feed were all gone. Then David's father would try to find a stubble field someplace, often a barley field.

David explains: *"Dad would like to get a field that had an irrigation ditch not too far away so that he wouldn't have to haul water. Down in the district there were lots of fields like that and the harvesting methods were fairly poor then so there was a lot just left lying on the ground. The turkeys would pick it up and eat it and they would eat the green grass off the edges of the ditch banks and they had water so it was a natural environment for them."*

Once the summer was over and turkey feed in the field was exhausted, the workers would haul all the turkeys to a rice field. They loaded the birds onto specially designed trucks that could hold about 500 turkeys each. Once they arrived at the rice field, releasing the turkeys from the truck was quite an event.

David remembers it well: *"I remember vividly seeing this. Good friends used to rent rice fields to Pa. I remember getting to the location, and the turkeys had their adult feathers but they were not totally grown. The turkeys are basically wild at this point; they could still fly. I remember opening those racks and the air was black with turkeys and sometimes they flew about a half mile!*

"The herder knew what to do. He took his dog and went and got them all together and brought them back. They were in a totally new environment and didn't know where home was. He had to establish a base for those turkeys. Every night he would bring them in. There was risk of wild animals, coyotes, and some would stray away. But generally the flock would stay together."

The entire process was about seven months, and usually in December the turkeys were prepared to go to market. The butchering camp was set up right where the turkeys were in the field.

David explains: *"They would set up a temporary facility with a rope with a piece of leather on the end of the rope, and they would hang the turkey by the feet and wrap it around twice and that leather piece would lock the turkey in. They had turkey pickers who just knew how to stick a turkey and cut its throat. Some of those guys could stick a turkey so that the feathers would almost fall off. There was a knack to it.*

"Now this was called a New York dress, they just took the feathers off, that's all they did, the intestines were still in and everything; they were just a hanging bird. It was generally done in late fall when it was cold. This was important because they had to get them cooled out. Pa used to put them right on the trucks and they would take them to San Francisco. They'd leave at three in the morning to take them so they would stay cool."

Another Mechanical Device

Two thousand turkeys was a large lot but the demand for Fiddyment poultry still could not be met. Russell knew he could sell more, but he wasn't sure how to do it economically. It was about 1938 and technology was about to provide him with the answer.

David tells the story: *"I remember the fellow just as if it was yesterday. He sat in the living room right on the couch and made a deal with my dad. He had heard that my dad was in the turkey business and he came to see him. He said he'd invented a mechanical brooder, a mechanical mother turkey. He sold Pa 60 gas brooders, and it was the first mechanical brooders that were sold in the United States.*

"I remember the stove, it was butane and butane had just come on the market. Dad would light the end of this tank and it would go to each of these brooders. Each little stove had a pilot light. The stove had a heat-sensitive wafer, and when it was fully expanded it pressed against the diaphragm that the gas was flowing through and would shut the gas off."

The stove was an ingenious invention! Russell adapted it easily into his operation.

David explains: *"Dad got together with another fellow and designed a portable building for the turkeys. It was designed after the idea of the mother hen in the field. He designed portable buildings with ten brooder stalls. It had a canvas top and each stall handled 400 baby turkeys.*

"The very day we would bring them from the hatchery they were confined to a brooder stove with a cardboard fence. The brooder stove provided the warmth and this took the place of the mother turkey. This new invention hatched 4,000 turkeys at a time. There were some anxious moments with all these babies just hatched! Everything had to be handled perfectly for the babies. My dad knew exactly what to do."

The babies required constant care. The heat had to be monitored, water and food had to be supplied.

And as David says: *"They didn't have a mother hen telling them (the babies) what to do so we'd have to show them."*

Once the babies grew large enough to roost outside their coops, the turkey herders began their process.

The brooder stove proved to be a great success, and Russell was able to satisfy the demand for Fiddyment turkeys. ❧

22

His First Love

The family ranch was a huge influence on David but at 16-years old, he had other interests as well. As a sophomore in high school he attended Roseville High and was finding that he had fun with other activities outside the ranch. He became involved in the high school band, and he was attracted to school politics and successfully ran for offices in student council. But his biggest love outside of the ranch had nothing to do with school; it had to do with an airplane.

David tells the story: *"Back in 1939 my brother Russ had graduated from San Rafael Military Academy and he came home and enrolled in Sacramento Junior College. I had admired the things that he accomplished, and I was intrigued by what he was doing. One of them was that he took a course on flying, which he called ground school. It was then that I decided I wanted to fly. I was a sophomore in high school, and I had just turned 16.*

"One day, September 13, I flew for eight hours with an instructor in the front seat of a two-seater Piper J-3 Cub. I started flying in this one and it didn't have any brakes on it. When we got on the ground it had a long runway and that thing would roll to a stop. After the eight

hours with an instructor he said just stop the airplane, I'm going to get out and you go ahead and fly it. Of course the thing that went through my mind was, 'Am I qualified to do this?' When the instructor was in the plane I had a sense of confidence that if anything had gone wrong he was certainly there to bail me out. Well with nobody in the front seat with me there was nobody to bail me out if something had gone wrong!

"But all I had to do was exactly what I did before, and I did! I flew it around, landed, flew it around, landed three or four times. I was flying solo eight hours after I learned to fly!

When he finally landed and got out of the airplane the instructor met him and told David he had passed. Now he was able to come in and get time for himself anytime he wanted, but he wasn't able to take anyone with him until he got his pilot rating.

Learning to fly was an experience that served David well his entire life. It eventually grew to be a large part of who he was, but his love had to wait. With the onslaught of trouble in Europe all recreational flying soon stopped. David wouldn't fly again until 1945.

Military Academy & the Decision

In high school David was grasping opportunities to try new things. He joined the band and tried trumpet and clarinet. He eventually got to be a pretty good drummer and was elected to the position of drum major in the band, and he played in the school orchestra where he found some great new friends. He grew to understand that his strengths were in science, math, chemistry, and physics. Foreign language was okay, and he just wasn't that good in English. He was voted in as the next class president with the choice of being student body vice president. But none of that was to be. The rattling sabers in Germany, Italy and Japan could be heard throughout the world. There was a war brewing and options for young men were changing.

Now David had a new choice, and he remembers it well: *"In 1941 I had an opportunity to go to San Rafael Military Academy. I thought gosh, if my mom and dad want to do that, it costs $1,500 but they said I could. So I packed up and they took me down on a Sunday afternoon. I showed them where my room was and everything and about 5:00 in the afternoon they said, 'Well, see ya later.' Well, I'd never left home before and it was like 'hello mudder, hello fadder, here I am at Camp Granader.' It wasn't long after they left that the bugler called for cadets to go to the mess hall.*

"Now I was involved in a whole new environment, and the best thing for me to do was to dive in with both feet and just do whatever had to be done. That made the transition from loneliness to being involved in a new way of life very short."

David finished his last two years of high school in the San Rafael Military Academy and overall it was an outstanding experience for him. As a military cadet he learned fast. He became a rifle marksman, learned how to make a bow and arrow and shoot it with precision, and graduated with an academic standing in the top 10 percent of the school.

He came home after San Rafael Military Academy and enrolled at UC Davis, an agricultural school at the time. As an extension of his academy training he became part of the ROTC program. He found that his classes were hugely helpful for his involvement on the ranch. Freshman year went without interruption, then in fall of his sophomore year, November of 1942, he received his draft notice.

David describes that time in his life as "a fork in the road." He knew he was a good military candidate because of his training at the military academy and ROTC training. His brother Russ was at UC Berkeley and had enlisted in the Naval Reserves, and his brother John had joined the Air Force. With both of his brothers gone as well as David, his father would be left to manage the ranch all on his own. It was a difficult decision but David decided to help his dad. He requested a deferment based on his involvement at the ranch and it was granted.

David reflects: *"I have no regrets about the fork in the road that I chose to take. My pa had the main objective to keep the family together. Growing turkeys was one way to do this. We were taught early on that today is the first day of the rest of our lives and to look back to grieve about what could or could not have happened wasn't productive at all."*

23

Roseville and WWII

War was imminent. Roseville's major employers responded quickly. In June of 1940 the city announced that any employees who were drafted would have their jobs waiting for them when they came home. At the same time, the railroad began making extensive modifications to accommodate the movement of thousands of troops and tons of military vehicles and supplies.

Then in October of 1940 local papers printed the notice that all men between the ages of 21 and 35 must register immediately for military service. The draft was on. In spring of the following year, Roseville High School opened classes for anyone interested in national defense work.

War came upon the nation quickly and the devastating blow of the bombing of Pearl Harbor put Roseville citizens into action immediately. The local police department formed the Civilian Defense Council, air raid alarms were installed, and bond drives began.

On a cloudy day in June of 1942 the good people of Roseville prepared to wave a tearful goodbye to some 200 young men as they signed up for the draft. In the course of the war, Roseville would send 1,250 of its young men and women off to fight. With the population at 6,653, a whopping 20 percent of its citizens were represented. It was a number considered one of the highest per capita ratios in the country.

While our military service members were a credit to Roseville, the labor force suffered. The railroad's Pacific Fruit Express had the greatest loss with about 25 percent of its labor force gone. Help was needed. Agreements were made to bring in workers from Native American groups and Mexican Nationals. In one of its innovative moments the railroad company modified old boxcars to help with housing. Women and high school students filled the gaps for jobs as they were able. Railroad employees worked shifts around the clock with overtime always available.

It was a strange time in our nation's history. We had just started to shake off the repercussions of the dark Depression years, now our young men and women were off fighting a horrific war. For the first time in a long while money could be earned easily, but all anyone really wanted was to bring their loved ones home. ∾

Russell Fiddyment makes good use of his flatbed truck during a wartime Roseville parade. The American flag and its symbolism is highlighted as "The Greatest Mother of All."

24

David Talks about His Father Russell

When David was granted the deferment and could now stay home to help with ranch duties, there was no doubt his father was relieved. His memories of his father are extensive and heartwarming.

He shares some of his thoughts: *"He was just a marvelous man. You know he didn't tell me things to do, he lived it and I observed and picked up what I learned from the way he did things. He just expected me to do them and know how to do them. Once in a while he'd offer suggestions, but he didn't require me to do things the way he wanted them done. There were no lectures.*

"He would take us with him; I had two other brothers and sometimes he'd take all of us. Those experiences were indelible.

"I guess to some degree that experience has stayed with me. I never had a job other than what I did on the ranch. He instilled in me the importance of being an individual, to be yourself, and I certainly appreciate that. I've

never expressed that in this manner but I loved my dad and the importance of having a good father cannot be over emphasized. I think he set a good pattern. I had enough common sense to follow it. There were also other things. There were certain things that had to be done, and we just did them.

"I remember when I was at UC Davis and during the first part of the war I came home with some ideas that I'd learned. He made a remark that to his knowledge they had never produced a band of turkeys that was marketable. They were always underfed or something was the matter with them. He didn't go to school, he didn't go past the 8th grade, although he did take a couple of courses at a business college in Sacramento; I think it was before he and my mom were married in 1920. At that time 8th grade prepared students for life if there were no specific subjects they were following. They learned how to read, they learned how to do math, they learned how to have good penmanship, how to write, how to construct a sentence properly, and those kinds of things were really about the only tools they needed. Unless

*Russell Frederick
Fiddyment*

*you wanted to be a doctor or
lawyer there wasn't any great need
for specialization. He was prepared
enough to do what had to be done.
I think in retrospect that he was not
shortchanged. He learned about
things through experience. He could
do them because he had the values
necessary to do them."*

25

The War Years on the Ranch

With deferment in place, David returned home to the ranch. One of the first tasks at hand was to address the business of the chicken operation. David and his brother had run the chicken operation together when they were in high school. Since his brother wasn't home and the business was expanding, David had to take it over.

He recalls: *"When I came home I took over the operation and started increasing egg sales. It was my job to do the planning, the marketing, and replace the hens with replacement stock. I had a nice route and produced enough eggs to supply all of Roseville and that worked very well. It gave me a little exposure that normally a farm boy wouldn't have. I got to know a lot of the merchants. At the same time I was working with my dad with turkeys and the sheep. It was a pleasure for me to help him."*

He goes on to explain: *"We had 1,200 laying hens, chickens, and they needed to have better housing. Dad decided to buy a piece of property next to us. It was 480 acres. This is where dad built the big chicken house. It was 400 feet long. We moved the chicken operation from over by the old ranch house to the new location."*

The numbers were astounding.

David remembers: *"My dad and I were in the turkey business at the time, and I was helping him. It was 1944 or maybe early 1945, the operation going on at this ranch was 4,000 laying (chicken) hens, 50,000 turkeys, a couple thousand breeder hens, 3,000 sheep. My father at this time was about 60-years old. There were very few growers who were that big at that time.*

"We had good opportunity during the war. There was a thing called price control that was intended to keep inflation from running rampant. It was the OPA: Office of Price Administration, and they would set the price for the commodities that we grew. With all of agriculture you knew what you were going to get from the outside. You could figure, if you didn't have some catastrophe in your business, you're going to make some money. It wasn't a lot but it was certainly more than you needed to start up for the next year.

"I remember when I was selling chicken eggs. I would check an association in Sacramento called the Poultry Producers, I would call them up every time I went in to market my eggs, and

The brooder house.

I would find out what the price of eggs was. They knew because the OPA had told them. There was an increment increase when it was light. When it's dark the chickens don't want to lay as many eggs. When it's light they lay more eggs. It's a logical thing. We'd fool them a little bit and turn the lights on. But the OPA did recognize that there was a reduction in supply and that should happen. When the supply is low the price goes up and when the supply is up the price goes down. It was a basic economic set of values. We knew what we could anticipate generally, it wasn't always exact. Same thing with the turkey industry.

"The war years were pretty well regulated by the Office of Price Administration. Supplies of some commodities were limited. Generally things were pretty much close to normal as you could get.

"You couldn't get tires, and you couldn't get gasoline. But the farmers were given preferential treatment. We had all the gasoline we needed. We could go to the place where we applied for our gasoline stamps, and if you were an average citizen you could get an A stamp

and that allowed for so many gallons of gas per week/per month. If you were in industry, and farming was one, you got the T stamps. We could call up our supplier, and the oil company was the supplier, and they would bring out 500 gallons of gas and we always had enough stamps to afford the purchase. I think gas was about 15 cents a gallon at that time. There was lots and lots of regulations and I think probably rightfully so."

David continues to share about the general state of the citizens: *"In the 1940's there was serious concern right after Pearl Harbor that the west coast was totally defenseless. There was nothing, by anyone in the armed services to have any kind of defense if the Japanese decided to have a landing party.*

"There was a civil defense department that asked us to set up a program. It was a program of spotters. The Fiddyments provided the building and the manning of the building 24 hours a day. They were to report every airplane that went by. The report had to include which

David Fiddyment prepares to deliver eggs into town.

direction, how high, one engine, two, night or day, etc. Mostly older people were spotters because there weren't very many around to do it. Bill Kaseburg was one of the spotters. The information went into an area where data was analyzed. If any of those sightings were an airplane that the military didn't know about then there was an alert.

"One day we got a report that one of these airplanes had crashed. It was a B-25 bomber. No one had any idea what happened, it just fell out of the sky. You can imagine the young trainees in these high-performance airplanes, most of them probably were not very skilled in what they were doing but there was a huge demand for pilots. I

guess they pushed them pretty hard. Once in a while one of these kids just couldn't hold it together and they'd stall out or run into somebody else. I don't know what happened, but this one crashed out there on Baseline Road about three miles from where our spotter house was.

"There was another one, a P-39. There was several of them coming toward McClellan Field and one of these crashed in the north part of the ranch.

"We all know the bottom line; eventually we were able to defeat all the aggressors. It was a real cost, World War II was a real tragedy.

"As far as my part was concerned I joined a local group call the CAP: Civil Air Patrol. We didn't have any equipment, but we were prepared in our basic groundwork to step in in the event that we were needed. Most of us had already had some flight training. We didn't know how it was going to apply but we went over to the high school, Don Pruitt and I, and ran this class for two or three years. Don was a Roseville neighbor and became a good friend.

It was Don who eventually got David back into flying. ❧

26

The Bellanca

It had not been his choice to stay away from flying, and as soon as the go-ahead from the government was given, he jumped at the opportunity to get back into an airplane. David's log book shows that it was July 10, 1945 that he started his training again. It had been a little over four years since he had passed his initial test, and he was anxious to earn his pilot's rating. As far as he was concerned he had been away from an airplane entirely too long.

The prerequisite for a pilot certificate was 35 hours of solo flying. On May 5, 1946, he passed the private pilot's flight test. Now he was ready for an airplane of his own.

With Don Pruitt's help he had ordered a plane that he really wanted, a Bellanca, but due to the war just being over there was a delay in getting it. By this time his brother Russ was home, so David, his brother, his father and cousin Walt all chipped in and bought a Taylor Craft airplane. David flew quite often and in November of 1946 his beloved Bellanca finally arrived.

In anticipation of getting the new airplane he had built a small airfield at the ranch. He had contracted a landing strip to be built, 1,800 feet long, running slightly up hill from the north to the south. He built a hangar.

David says: *"When the Bellanca came I remember picking that airplane up and I had never flown one before. It was quite the departure from the Taylor Craft. But the controls were basically the same so I just got in it and flew it. Seating was the same, controls were with the wheel, instruments basically the same, but it was a much higher performing airplane. It would go about 150 miles per hour while the other airplane went about 90 miles per hour. It was a low-wing airplane however, the others were high wing and it also had retractable landing gear. Those things I had to kind of figure out. It wasn't long before I spent an hour and 30 minutes."*

David continued to fly; both for work and for pleasure. One particular trip was especially memorable.

David shares the story: *"The Bellanca was just an outstanding airplane. One time my dad and I were headed back from a trip toward the valley, and I asked him if he wanted to fly. He was sitting on the right side and I dozed off. Here he was flying this airplane and not knowing what to do. Pretty soon he was giving me the nudge and he said, 'What'd I do?' and he had the airplane in a dive going about 200 miles an hour!"*

David laughingly recalls: *"We got it straightened out."*

27

Extracurricular Opportunities

Throughout the course of their lives, David and Dolly were both involved in numerous philanthropic pursuits. David's entre' into the world of giving back began early on in his career. It actually started several years before he was married. He shares some of his experiences.

20/30 Club

"In 1946 the 20/30 Club in Roseville had a project to recognize young farmers. It was a project that was statewide. Someone said, 'Can I submit your name for Young Farmer of the Year? I said, 'Sure!' So we had an interview, and when the tally was made I was elected for the county. I was third runner-up of all the young farmers in the entire state!"

4-H Club

In 1946 David and friend Don Pruitt began the first 4-H Club in the Dry Creek area of Roseville. They ran the club for six years before handing it off to new leadership. The 4-H Club is still strong in Roseville today.

Placer County Fair Board

"The 20/30 Club award opened up a lot of things for me. The fair board wanted me, and I was on the board with 40- and 50-year olds. I felt like it was such an honor." David served on the fair board for 30 years.

Placer County Agricultural Commission

David served as commissioner for 10 years. It was an effort that included the protection of agriculture land and ensuring the land was taxed properly.

Rotary Club

"A fellow I had gotten to know in town was a member of the Rotary Club; Hal Wentworth. Hal asked me to come and visit the club, and he had turned in an application on my behalf and I didn't know about it. Well the next thing you know I was a member of the Roseville Rotary Club! That was 1947. I went into Rotary on May 10, 1947 and here I was only 24-years old. That was unheard of because most who were in that club were middle-aged and older. At that time it was considered to be an old man's club.

"In retrospect I didn't really realize the full implication or responsibility of what I was accepting. It's intended to be a philanthropic organization for the community. Well I had a pretty good business so I was able to keep up my end of the bargain. In retrospect I think had I not been included as an equal in that community that my whole life would have been different. I got to know people. I got to know things that generally were good business practices. I learned how to conduct a meeting and learned what was important. It gave me insight to a life that I had never known before. I guess it was the process of planning, cooperation, learning how to engage people, get them to be part of the team; all of those things are part of the process. I don't think you get that going through school. I'm eternally grateful for having that opportunity."

Fiddyment Farms

Proudly Recognizes

DAVID FIDDYMENT

For *Sixty* years of attendance and service for the

Rotary Club of Roseville

"Rotary has been a very fulfilling experience in my life. I'm in full agreement with the many projects it has undertaken. The potential for doing even more is huge. The relationship with the other members of the community is also very rewarding to me personally. I like to be involved and I thank Rotary for the wonderful privilege.

David Fiddyment

David Fiddyment has had a lifetime commitment to agriculture and the environment. Nearly forty years ago, Mr. Fiddyment began the farming, production and distribution of pistachios grown on his farm. Due to David's innovative design and ingenuity, today, Fiddyment Farms is one the most well-established local companies in the Placer County area. David has also been a valued member of the Rotary Club of Roseville in which he is honored for his perfect attendance and wonderful service.

28

A Young Lady Named Dolly

It is appropriate that David was involved with his first love, his airplane, when he met the woman he would marry. Their story is very sweet and has a memorable twist.

David tells it with expression that only a sweetheart's love can bring: *"My sister Coralie had enrolled in UCLA and was staying in Los Angeles to go to school. A friend of mine and I decided that we would go down for a visit to see my sister. On July 12, 1947, we flew down and landed in a little airport out at Culver City. My sister knew I was coming but she had a date with a fellow, and she asked her roommate to go down and meet me.*

"So here this young lady came when I had landed there, and she came up to the airplane and introduced herself as Dolly Lorenzen."

Dolly Fiddyment, second from the left, hosts a birthday party for her son, mid-1950s.

Newly married David and Dolly Fiddyment.

David doesn't say it, but at this point in the interview it's clear he knew right away that Dolly was a special lady. He spent the day and evening with her, his sister, and a group of friends. They had a lovely time.

"We flew back the next day. Then a week later I flew back to Los Angeles again and I had a date with Dolly, which kind of started things. I did a lot of flying back and forth.

"Then on August 8th I flew into Huntington Beach. That was Dolly's home. Then I was making pretty regular trips going to Huntington Beach.

"On November 2nd Dolly was with me and we flew out to Long Beach. We were out there for an hour and 15 minutes. We flew over the Long Beach Harbor and down there on the water was this huge, huge flying boat that Howard Hughes had built, the Spruce Goose! It was taxiing around and you could see the boat wake in the water. All of a sudden that wake disappeared and it was flying! And it flew for about maybe a mile, mile and a half, then he settled it back down. We saw the Spruce Goose fly!"

"Later on that summer Dolly came up to Roseville by car. Mom was up at the cabin, our summer home, and we went up there sometime in August. At that point I just decided that she was the lady I wanted to spend the rest of my life with. We were up in the mountains and I asked her to marry me. And she said she would. I met her on the 12th of July 1947 and we were married on the 17th of February of '48. We were married in Huntington Beach."

In a conversation many years later Dolly would say about David, *"He literally flew into my life."* ❧

Dolly Fiddyment

David Fiddyment & Dolly Lorenzen m. 1948

|
Duane
Deborah
Diane

29

Fiddyment Brothers

"My sons – David, Russell Jr., and John, really run the business now." – Russell Fiddyment, *Roseville Press Tribune* Article, 1948

After the war the brothers John and Russ were back in Roseville. Both of them had also gotten married, and the three brothers had all established their own homes on the ranch. They formed the Fiddyment Brothers business in 1945. David's chicken and egg business was still lucrative so he continued working in both.

The business of bringing turkeys to the consumer market was changing and each time something new was introduced, the brothers worked together to modify their operation. In this way they were able to keep their facilities as modern as possible. It was a very different operation from where it began.

David shares: *"Now the turkey hen did nothing*

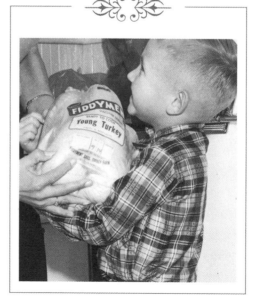

more than lay eggs. Those eggs were hatched in an incubator, then a mechanical brooder stove was used to keep the babies warm. Once they were large enough we would put all the babies in large pens and fed them mechanically."

Indeed it was a different process, and the laws were changing too. Butchering turkeys became a little more complicated.

"… my dad had just butchered them in the field, but things were changing and the laws didn't want us to do that."

David continues to explain: *"The idea to build a plant just for butchering turkeys was a new idea, and my dad was very interested."*

Nephew Eric Fiddyment is excited to hold the Thanksgiving turkey.

Turkey processing from beginning to end.

The brothers were fortunate to locate a plant for sale that was specifically designed for butchering turkeys. They bought the equipment and moved it all into a modified old barn on the ranch. It was immediately put it into operation. The newest part of the Fiddyment Brothers business was a success.

David recalls: *"The process involved in this plant was the scalding method as opposed to the dry method of picking a turkey. That brought a whole different set of conditions into the end result."*

In an article written for the *Roseville Press-Tribune* published on November 19, 1948, David's father Russell describes the steps of the processing plant to a reporter: *"They bring the turkeys in that door. They put one turkey foot on one side of this thing, the other foot on the other side, then the feet are secured with spring clamps."*

The reporter describes the scene in front of him: *"Hanging head down the turkeys move on down the line until they reach the spot where a man with a knife deftly cuts the throat."*

The reporter goes on to write: *"Moving along, the fowl gets a dip in a vat of 122-degree water and from there it passes through a mechanical picker that takes off most of the feathers – an enormous time-saving operation. The fowl is then transferred to another set of dangling loops and the remainder of the picking is done. After*

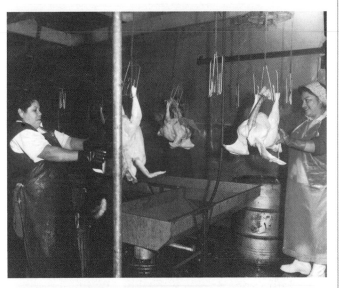

The finished product.

that the turkey is placed in a rack that holds 80 hens. There it is washed with a hose and once the rack is full, it is pushed aside to allow the turkeys to dry off. The neck of the fowl is next wrapped in white butcher's paper and the bird is ready for the cooler."

Eventually the brothers incorporate a thorough eviscerating step into the process. A little later on, shrink-wrap is included and each turkey is marketed with the Fiddyment Brothers name and logo proudly printed on the wrapper. The Fiddyment Brothers partnership eventually produces a turkey that is oven-ready for the consumer.

The brothers were in business together roughly 10 years, from 1945 to 1955. In the duration of those years the industry changed dramatically. More and more growers were coming to Placer County, health laws were changing that mandated stringent regulations, and the

biggest hurdle of all was introduced to the turkey business: the union.

The unions became the final blow.

David elaborates: *"The union came in and said you can't sell to a union shop unless you are a union shop. They said when it came to marketing the product if we didn't have union help butchering the products we couldn't sell to a union butcher. We began to realize with the demands the union was placing on us we could not do what we had to do and still be able to compete. It was an economic decision from our standpoint.*

We could have met the health department requirements with some major changes. But we realized in the long run it wasn't in our best interest so we decided we weren't going to continue with the finished product to the consumer."

It had been a productive and profitable time but it no longer could be a viable business. The brothers decided to opt out of the turkey-processing business. But they did continue the Fiddyment hatchery, and David continued his chicken and egg business.

David talks about the hatchery: *"We produced turkey-hatching eggs. We hatched the baby turkeys and sold them as baby turkeys, and we called it the Fiddyment Hatchery and it was part of Fiddyment Brothers. My brother Russ liked to do the selling. We sold baby turkeys to growers around the area.*

"I recall one Thanksgiving the whole family was over at my mom's place and the hatch was ready to come off. It takes 28 days for the turkey egg to hatch, and we had put them in incubators. For 25 days they were in the incubator and for the last three days they had to be transferred to another part of the hatchery unit that was the hatching side of it. There they stayed for the last three days and in the process the little baby turkeys were hatching out of these eggs. They were in trays, and the trays were covered so the little babies couldn't pop out. So we had these trays and we'd open up a tray and there would be 300 little turkeys look up at you; cutest little things. (On that Thanksgiving) we had to transfer them from there into boxes that held about a 100 turkeys each. There they stayed until we shipped them out to growers.

The timing of the turkey hatch had made it a memorable Thanksgiving. Sadly though, it was likely the last Thanksgiving David's father, Russell Sr., was present. He passed away February 14, 1956. He was 69-years old.

Without her husband, Cora felt her sons should entirely take over the business. Months after Russell's death, Cora sold the section of the ranch that contained the majority of the turkey buildings and equipment to David's brother, John. John had decided to continue with the turkey business in a big way.

At this point David was easing himself out of the poultry business altogether.

He explains: *"On my own I had a little side business, I had several thousand chickens. They were called broiler or fryer chickens as opposed to laying hens. I had used the processing plant to do the marketing of those chickens. It was not a major business and the union never did come and tell me I couldn't do it. I only had a couple of people working for me. We sold chickens to all the markets in the Roseville area along with eggs I was selling to them. That worked fine for a while but it gradually got to a point where the income from them wasn't worth the effort. So I decided to stop."*

30

The Next Many Years

It was 1956 and the land that David owned was not being utilized. He took some time to reflect on his decision to get out of the poultry business.

He shares his thoughts: *"There came a time in my life when I realized it wasn't what I really wanted to do. The risks were high; the remunerations were low."*

The road ahead was not clear, but he needed to continue on to help support his family.

"Not knowing what I was going to do, we had a family, and fortunately Dolly decided to teach school and help with the finances. There was a couple of years where I did odd jobs.

"I bought a rice harvester one fall, and I harvested rice on a contract basis for some of the rice growers. I tried growing clover, that wasn't successful; the water supply costs were too high. I used some of my land for growing watermelons and squash and when my dad willed me 80 acres there was a vineyard on the property, and it had been planted prior to the time my dad bought it in 1941. One part of that vineyard could have gone back 60 or

70 years. There were big, big grapevines. They were of a variety that wasn't very popular, mission variety. I produced that vineyard for a couple of years then we got into a disease and it had an effect on the vineyard and the production kept getting less and less. I finally got to the point where I pulled it out. I used the ground for a couple of other things too, neither of those worked."

After about 10 years of doing various odd jobs, David happened upon an article that would change the course of his life. ❧

Dolly Fiddyment takes her kindergarten class on a tour of the Fiddyment family ranch. (right)

A grove of trees on the Fiddyment property. Photo courtesy of Jim Peters. (below)

31

Death of Russell Fiddyment Sr.

When Russell passed away the Roseville paper ran it as front-page news. A man of his stature, coming from a family that had been in the area for over 100 years, was indeed newsworthy. The article's first sentence states, "Roseville lost one of its most widely-known pioneer residents last night…" It goes on to say, "Mr. Fiddyment died on the same ranch where he was born 69 years ago. … Although widely known in Roseville itself, Mr. Fiddyment centered his activities around his ranch and rural life."

He lived through some of the world's most historical events, and all the while he worked for the sole purpose of keeping the family's business going so his children could continue the legacy. His father began teaching him to work the ranch from the time he could walk. It became the work he loved and would stay in all his life. At 69-years old, he left this world early, especially compared to his father and his grandmother's lives.

His children called him "Pa" all their lives and dearly loved him for the strong, caring role model his was. Russell Fiddyment was a critical part of the Fiddyment legacy and his memory stays with the family to this very day. ❧

The death of Russell Fiddyment makes front page headline news.

32

The Nut Tree

Instinctively David knew that the right choice for him was to get out of the turkey business. It was a good choice. Eventually the industry moved out of Placer County almost entirely. He also knew that he had 25 acres of good soil, and he needed to figure out how to make it profitable. Several attempts had been made but success was yet to come. In the meantime he was utilizing his harvester to do odd jobs, all the while knowing in the back of his mind something had to come of the land.

Late in 1968 an idea presented itself. An intriguing article in a magazine for farmers, "California Cultivator," caught his eye. A new crop that had never been grown in the US was being tested, and the US Department of Agriculture was spearheading the effort. The illusive crop was a nut tree, and it was unlike any nut tree that had ever been grown on American soil. The crop was pistachio nuts.

The US Department of Agriculture had tried to grow pistachio trees the same way other fruit and nut trees were grown in the US. This was the bare-root planting method in nursery rows. That didn't work very well as only five percent of the trees survived. However, there was a nursery in Corning that was having some success. They were growing them in containers until they were good-sized seedlings, and then transplanting them into the soil.

David gave the nursery owners a call and, hearing what they had to say, thought this might actually be a crop that could work on his land.

He recalls: *"So I decided to buy a few trees and see what would happen. I didn't want to jump in 100 percent right off the bat. I bought 360 trees and planted two acres. It was January of 1969."*

The trees arrived. The next day as he was digging in the dirt, an exchange occurred that was to stay with him his entire life. A neighbor, a fellow he had known quite a while, was driving past and spotted David. When he saw David making the holes in the ground with hundreds of tree seedlings nearby, he stopped his car and loudly inquired, "Dave, what the hell are you doing out there?" David told him. The man replied, "You won't live long enough to see those things come into production." David then said, "John, I think you're right—unless I do it and it succeeds.. You only find out if you try." David continued planting his pistachio seedlings.

Fiddyment pistachio orchard.

oranges were already well-planted crops, pistachios became the new darling.

This left all supplies of seedlings not only depleted, they were now contracted out for the next several years. This left David in a quandary; he remembers the moment well: *"When he told me he couldn't supply me with any more seedlings I asked, 'What am I going to do?' He said, 'Why don't you grow your own?'"*

David didn't have the slightest idea of what to do in terms of growing nursery seedlings. He was a turkey farmer. But not one to be easily defeated, he went to the US Department of Agriculture station in Chico and ordered seeds. While he was waiting for the delivery he began to prepare.

He recalls: *"I realized my inadequacy so I went back to school, nights, three nights a week. I built a little greenhouse and got a few ideas on what to do."*

He attended classes at Sierra College and ended up staying in school for the next five years. He studied irrigation, soils, and anything related to food crops. He learned a lot of things, one of which was that the pistachio is quite the fickle seed.

It does not grow as a normal tree seed in that you can't plant it into the ground and then have a seedling immediately sprout. The problem is nature designed the pistachio tree to live 400 to

The trees did take hold and by the next year his little orchard was doing well. With gained confidence from his success, David decided he would plant a full 10 acres of the pistachio seedlings. He returned to the nursery to buy more but there was a problem.

David recalls: *"I went up to talk to Ken and he said he couldn't sell me a tree for five years. I asked what the heck happened? Ken said "the IRS."*

It was a new wrinkle. The IRS had been instructed by Congress to be kind to growers of certain types of permanent agricultural crops. Oranges, grapes and pistachios were on the list. The IRS had changed the rules for these growers so they could write off expenses upfront instead of waiting to capitalize and depreciate over time. The bottom line was that cash-rich companies, like the Superior Oil Company near Bakersfield, started buying land to plant orchards. Since grapes and

Dave Fiddyment of Roseville is one of California's leaders in the blossoming pistachio nut industry. At right, unlike other nuts, pistachios grow in clusters. As the trees get larger and older, the clusters are closer together on the tree and also heavier, thus increasing the yield of each tree.

PISTACHIO NUTS
This Long-Time "Comer" May Be About to Arrive

500 years. They're an ancient crop and are indigenous to the Middle East. Pistachio nuts are even mentioned in the bible as one of the gifts Pharaoh sent to Egypt. But that's another story.

The pistachio seed has an extremely thick seed coat and to get the embryo to break through is quite a process. Nature knows best. If these trees live hundreds of years then how many seedlings are necessary? The success rate of five percent is likely the natural process. But David needed to start an orchard and the natural process was not going to work. He had to figure out how to force the seeds into sprouting.

He describes the options: *"The first thing is you have to reduce the thickness of the seed coat. You could rub it off with sand paper or you could use acid to eat away the outer layer of seed coat. I tried both. The scarification method was difficult, it was hard to know how long to rub. The acid treatment, sulfuric acid, we found we could pour acid on the*

seed and they would immediately get hot and we left it on a certain period of time. That made it easy for water to penetrate and get the process going."

It worked! David successfully grew and planted pistachio tree seedlings on his property. It appeared that he finally found a use for his land that could be profitable.

It was the end of the year in 1969 and life was taking a new turn for David and Dolly Fiddyment. Along with their success in planting pistachio trees, a few years earlier in 1965 the couple had the opportunity to add a wonderful new member to their family. He was a young Farm School graduate from Greece who wanted an American family to help further his education about farming. The Fiddyments jumped at the opportunity. Bill Evangelou arrived at David and Dolly's house on December 23, 1965. The 1960's were bringing positive connections into their lives. ✎

33

Bill Evangelou

He arrived with little knowledge of the language or the customs, but David and Dolly welcomed the 18-year old with open arms. He was in America to learn. His desire was to become an agricultural engineer, and he felt to be successful he needed to complete his education in the United States. The young man had a lot to learn.

David remembers well: *"This was 1965, Diane was nine-years old. We got him on December 23. His only English was Greek translated into English words, he wasn't thinking in English yet. He was very willing to chip in, with most things. One of the things we did after dinner was jump up and clean up, but this was offensive to him. To Bill, that was not man's work, it was women's. It kind of bothered him but he pitched in with everybody else. Later, when he went back to visit his home town (in Greece) and cleared up the table, his mother said what are you doing, men don't do this!"*

But he came to them with an open mind. He wanted to learn. Dolly and David counseled with the high school and all agreed it would benefit Bill to learn the language. He had graduated from the American Farm School in Greece but his language skills were still very poor. So they enrolled him into high school and he attended for about a year and a half. He made the transition; he went in as a Greek and came out with a good understanding of what it was to be American.

David recalls: *"At first he was possibly frightened because of the new things, the uncertainty. But he was willing to charge ahead. We helped him in any way we could to help reduce the uncertainty. Bill and Diane hit it off tremendously, and I think he felt more at home just because of the relationship with our kids."*

Theirs was a wonderful relationship. Bill appreciated the Fiddyment family, and the family enjoyed him and his ambitions to be successful. They worked well together. One year, in 1972 David, his son Duane, and Bill put their heads together to build a dam on Pleasant Grove Creek. David needed water to irrigate his newly planted pistachio trees. It was quite an effort.

David recalls the scene: *"With Bill we built the forms, the steel-structure plates, and poured about 100 yards of concrete. Bill was there all the time and so was Duane (his son). Duane was about 23- or 24-years old."*

The dam was built, and it served the family's efforts for many years. Bill was instrumental in its design and building.

When the dam was built Bill was attending Sierra College. His studies went well and he easily graduated. His next step was Chico State. During those college years in Chico he met a beautiful young lady by the name of Shelly. Theirs was a destined love and even though Bill was young, 22, they were married.

His time in America was overall a brilliant success. David and Dolly accepted him as a son and were hugely proud of him.

As David recalls his memories of this young man he is smiling with a sparkle in his eye: *"Bill had a huge desire. He had teaching ability. Everyone loved that accent, the Greek-American accent. He decided to enroll at UC Davis and go into soil science. He graduated with a doctor's degree. He went to the highest plateau! He was offered a teaching position at University of Kentucky as an Associate Professor in soil science. His papers were getting published so he decided to write books. He wrote a book on pistachios, the history, culturing, food stock, all those things. We still have his books."*

Bill went on to earn a very prestigious position as Director of Soils at the State University at Ames Iowa. He and Shelly had two beautiful children, a boy and a girl. Because of David and Dolly, Bill was able to realize an excellent start to his career, be a great contributor to agriculture in the United States, and start a wonderful family.

They kept in touch over the years and once Bill's family moved to Iowa David and Dolly made plans for a visit. But before they could make the trip, a sad phone call came from Shelly. Bill had died suddenly from a heart attack. It was 2003. He was 56-years old. David and Dolly are still in close contact with Shelly. Their relationship will always share the bond of the wonderful boy who came from the Greek islands to learn farming in America. ✎

34

Time Goes On

Prior to the 1970s all America's pistachios came from Iran. While the red-stained nut treat was mildly popular, there was never a real interest to learn how to produce them in the States. But in the '70's that outlook was to change.

For David everything was coming together. In addition to going to school, he did extensive research through a partnership with the University of California at Davis. He performed wide-ranging experiments to understand diseases and the best variety of tree for disease resistance. It is likely some of his test trees are still growing on his original acreage. The climate, the soil, and the farmer—it was all working.

Other pistachio crops around the state weren't doing quite as well. Some orchards were planted in old cotton ground and disease wiped out the trees, while others planted varieties that didn't do well in colder weather. Many would-be pistachio farmers turned away when they learned the tree is a taproot plant; a delay crop. In these plants the root grows first, then the tree. Everyone was learning that to get a viable pistachio tree seedling and subsequent orchard, it took skilled effort and time.

Once the seedlings are growing the wait isn't over. Pistachio trees take a good four, sometimes five years before they begin to produce, and as the tree ages it produces larger amounts and better quality nuts. All in all the time to realize an actual income that clears expenses is relatively long. Most farmers want their return on investment in a much shorter period. But David instinctively knew success, and he is a patient man.

By 1971 David had proven to be one of the few successful pistachio growers in the state, and by 1973 his example was widely known. The demand for seedlings exploded. Now was David's chance to finally put his land into a real income-producing mode.

He was growing the trees and successfully selling seedlings. The orchard he started and expanded upon was thriving. By 1974 his nursery business was thriving. It was confirmation that his new venture was the right choice.

By 1976 his pistachio crop was large enough that he needed to invest in his own machinery for processing. It was another milestone and turning point in his and Dolly's lives.

He bought a peeler, a crude one compared to what was to evolve, and he built his own dryer. Peeling and hulling was initially a challenge but with some ingenuity and some testing of different machine designs, David accomplished his goals. In addition to his successful orchard, he was now in the pistachio processing business.

David processed the nuts from his own land as well as some of the biggest orchards in southern California. His machinery was advanced for its time, and pistachio tree growers recognized David as "the" area processor. At the time he was able to produce 300,000 to 500,000 pounds of nuts in a season, but it wasn't near what was possible.

David recognized the potential for a very lucrative business so he kept designing and creating new ways for processing to be efficient. He explained it was a mental process, and that his days of turkey farming had prepared him well for the exercise.

Finding success in the pistachio business is overall a complicated business, and processing the nuts can be especially tricky. It all has to be done in a timely manner or the product quickly deteriorates and the whole crop is lost. David did a lot of testing. There were some failures in his initial designs, but the challenges were overcome. David realized victory in both the growing and the processing of pistachios.

Over the course of the next 30 years, David was to make major contributions to the pistachio farming industry. He eventually developed a nut processor that hulls and dries pistachios just moments from the time they are harvested. He designed a roaster and equipment that is specifically designed to separate the nuts for quality.

There is a tremendous amount of labor that goes into taking the pistachio from seed to shelf, and David figured it out. Pistachio growing in California is successful largely because of David's involvement and efforts. ᓚ

35

The Land Changes

David's brother John stayed in the turkey business until May 1988, and the last of his sheep were sold in the fall of 1991. He had started into a four-year process to sell his portion of Fiddyment land in 1989, and in 1992 all of his land was cleared and Del Webb broke ground for the Sun City Roseville community.

David continued to grow and process pistachios on his property until 2002. At that time he and remaining family members living on Fiddyment land completed a sale to a developer.

Wanting to stay in the pistachio business, David and Dolly exchanged their Roseville interest for another orchard in Kern County. It is an older, larger orchard, a farm that was begun long ago as a nursery that provided seedlings to some of those cash-rich oil companies. The headquarters for their business, Fiddyment Farms, is now in Lincoln. Every year their southern California orchard produces more and more pistachios.

Planting those little seedlings in 1965 turned out to be the right thing to do after all.

It has been well over 150 years since the day Elizabeth Jane and her husband started a cattle ranching empire in West Roseville. Her son Walter grew up on her land and witnessed some of the world's biggest changes. Walter's son Russell worked through the changes and ensured the family business stayed intact. Russell's son David was the last to make a living off the land that his ancestors settled so long ago.

Today David sees hundreds of homes in place where his family legacy was created. Asking him about his thoughts is a bittersweet moment. David sums up his feelings in one simple phrase:

"The land may change but the history never will." ❧

The ranch house as it looks today.

I Feel So Blessed in the Life I Had

A Tribute to Duane Fiddyment

David and Dolly's first-born, Duane Martin Fiddyment, left this world on July 28, 2013. This author had the fortunate opportunity to interview Duane in March of 2012. The following excerpts from his interview show us that his childhood was very much like his ancestors who lived before him.

The House Duane Grew Up In

"The house that I grew up in was a two- or three-room house at first, and there were several remodels. The first one was dad taking off the back porch, moving the laundry room from the back porch, and extending south to make the living room and dining room. On the end of the kitchen was a breakfast nook, and it had two or three fairly big windows that looked west and were shaded by a big oak tree. To the south of the nook there was an open porch, and a lean-to roof and two or three steps that came from the porch down to the patio area. As the family grew so did the house.

"We never had a junk pile, we had a burn barrel. We'd take the trash out, fill the burn barrel up, light it, and let it burn down. If it got too full we'd empty the burn barrel. There must have been a low spot up by the creek where we'd take it. You know in that part of the world you figure out that least desirable piece of real estate and use it for a dumping ground.

"The well that we used was that big well. The well to the north of the mill, this is the one that has the big galvanized pressure tank, the one that fed all the facilities there. There was a fairly big pipe that came down [from it] past the mill and it had a pipe on the corner. That was the place where, when you were hot, you could get a really cold drink of water because the valve was at about three feet, you know sort of like it was your drinking fountain. You would wash your face and rinse buckets out."

Learning from His Father

"I remember my dad as being this young, virile guy with really dark hair, and a really nice smile. Dad's belief about what you know is what you figure out on your own. You pay attention to what's going on in your environment so you learn from that. He encouraged the self-motivation. At that stage I don't recall ever being chastised or punished for something I would do.

"I liked working with my dad. I've always liked working with him. This is it, I'm paying attention to what he's doing and I anticipate what he needs next. He appreciated that. That's the ethic he was looking for. There's nothing that was specific about what he said, he'd always say you figure it out, you know what to do, just do it."

Mom (Dolly)

"Mom came from Huntington Beach, an urban environment; so coming out to this rural place was a pretty big shock. Mom has a story about eating mushrooms for the first time at gram's house. She said she almost threw up when she saw this tureen full of black liquid with slimy mushroom caps floating in it. She was the person of honor for that particular day and that was the family dish. I don't think she ever prepared that for us.

"Mom would insist on taking me to Sunday school at the Presbyterian Church, across Dry Creek. I remember the Sunday school classrooms. We didn't do Bible study per se. I don't have any strong memories but I think Deborah excelled at it. I don't think we were in competition, but I did feel a great sense of accomplishment when I could name all of the books of the bible. What mom was doing, my feelings, I always felt very safe and cared for.

"We would get together with all the cousins when we'd go to gram's, for dinner or whatever, and Christmas, Thanksgiving and Easter were big deals. As a young child I remember mom and the sister-in-laws would put on Easter egg hunts. There was a lot of squealing and laughing. There was a tradition of finding a golden egg and there was some kind of prize if you got it. All these cousins were out there scrambling around trying to find this thing. This was an annual event and I can remember it through high school.

"Mom would read stories to us about the bunny with the golden egg. It was a great kids story. I think we used mom's copy to read to the boys (his grandchildren)."

Playtime

"What I recall, and I'm probably 10, 11, 12 at this point, is that Dad would run the well for a certain number of hours every day to water the pasture. He would make a ditch in the ground that was probably three feet wide and maybe a foot deep. When the water would come out of the well it was just crystal clear and cold – 54 degrees probably. The water spilled out of the output pipe and it would run down this ditch.

"For me this was a lot of fun because I would make boats and sail them! I'd make the boats out of all sorts of stuff; plastic models, wood models, whatever I could get my hands on. One time I remember I made a plastic model, and one of my buddies had access to firecrackers. So I had a bomb, a fireworks bomb! We put it in the model and lit it, and let it float down the river, and it blew up! You know it was a very spectacular thing! You know, it was a boy thing!"

The Train Set

"I have a Lionel train set, the bigger one, that dad bought me. He set it up around the base of the Christmas tree in the living room. Here this train arrives and I was flabbergasted! I was not old enough to really comprehend how it worked or how to control it very well. Mom told me later he got it because he wanted it!

"Dad made the point that this is yours but you have to take care of it. We got the newspaper when we started to clean up after Christmas, and we wrapped each car up individually and packed them away in the box. We only used it at Christmas time but later on I used it more often.

"I did do something that maybe a lot of boys would have done; I decided to see what it could do as a battering ram. I laid out a bunch of straight track, made a wall out of some blocks, and crashed the engine into the wall. A couple of pieces broke off. I damaged my toy! I think dad was disappointed that I wasn't taking care of my stuff. There weren't any consequences, but I recognized that I did something stupid. I felt bad."

The Lay of the Land

"It was all very open. Patches of trees along the creek, a few solitary trees in the fields, dry grass in the summertime, green velvet in the spring and early summer. In late winter the animals that were there, whether they were turkey or they were sheep, I'd notice them. By that time I was in school and mom was insistent that I do my homework. I pushed back on that, she'll tell you, I would have rather been outside.

"In the springtime there were poppies, and fairy rings around the oak trees. A fairy ring is a mushroom grouping that tends to be in a circle and it pops up when there's a first rain of the year.

"Pleasant Grove Creek is a weir runoff stream, meaning in the summer time it's bone dry, in the winter time there's runoff water from the surrounding area. It's a watershed. It was only about a quarter of a mile north of the house. I think I made some play forts, or some hidey-holes along there at different times. The trees are huge, and I did build a fairly elaborate structure in the cross of the big tree that was right behind our house.

"I remember one of the trees that was in the tributary had a very unusual root structure and we played on that. Think about the Hobbits – that's what it reminds me of. Gnarly little thing, things looping around, you could crawl underneath it. It was huge for me as a kid.

"I remember being down in Pleasant Grove Creek when it was a dry, big sandy bottom, and walking down the creek west until we got to north of gram's house, then walking up past the runway and going to her house. It was something we would do from time to time rather than walk down Fiddyment Road or head out cross-country through the turkey pens and all of that. It was mostly grassland. There were trees along the waterways and disbursed trees out in the prairie.

"The thing about that ground out there is that when you look at it from a distance it seems flat, but when you walk through it there are undulations, and it's the way the water sculpted the land to get to its runoff point, its lowest point, to get to Pleasant Grove Creek.

"Later on, where Fiddyment Road used to cross Pleasant Grove Creek, as you go east, there were two forks that came together. The piece of property between those two forks, back to the east edge of dad's property, had a little piece of ground. I would call it the island. It would be used for picnics or annual events for dad's Rotary Club. My Scout Troop, Troop 61, went there several times for campouts. That was a lot of fun. It was great for me because that was my property!

"The island was a place that had special significance. Later on we changed it because of business necessities. We planted seedling pistachios there, and we used the dirt for pot-filling material so it changed from its original nature or contours. It made me sad that we did that, but I understood why we did it. It was a resource that we could exploit and so we did."

The Feed Mill

"There was a process of mixing up the feed before we took it out [to the turkeys]; we did it in the mill. The mill was this great big building and it had three or four huge grain cribs.

"The mill was our way of making our own feed. We'd buy the raw product, the grains and meal and all of the things that we'd use in the turkey feed.

"There would be a formula for what the feed was going to be, and I'd usually be working with dad and we would be just in there making up batches of feed. It wasn't every day but it was fairly frequent. We'd spend half a day making the batch of feed, and it would be half an hour to deliver it. We fed the turkeys less than every day.

"All of this was always there as far as I can remember. It had to have been something that Grandpa and Uncle Russ and Uncle John and dad had to have built at some point early on. It was probably the 1940's or 1930's that it was manufactured.

"That whole process of mixing the feed up instead of buying it outright was a cost savings. Everything in my recollection, everything we did on the ranch, was to not be wasteful, to be frugal, to use things and repurpose them."

The Turkeys

"There was another building that was used for growing out turkeys – it was the nursery. It's this very long building that had pens on either side, with a storage facility, and a cooler and big walk-in icebox.

"The thing I remember about this building was they would bring in wood shavings, except down the middle it was clear. There were warming hoods that were suspended from the rafters; they looked like a wide conical cap. They had infrared heaters in the top for the turkey chicks. It was a warming hat.

"So the process was, put the ring up, and put the feeding trays out and water cans. Let the chicks out, light the infrared heater, it was a surrogate mother.

"They would expand their living space as the baby turkeys got bigger. Once they got to be a pound or two we could put them outside. Outside that building there were pens attached to the building. Once they outgrew that they could be turned out into the fields. Then we would use the feeding process described earlier.

"There were pens from about a half-mile west of our house all the way over to about a half-mile east of gram's house, along the Pleasant Grove Creek waterway.

"When we stopped the turkeys it was a hard time financially. There was just no money in it unless you went big. Uncle John decided to go big. The land was repurposed, and he built giant, big and open buildings and he raised the birds very similarly, with the exception that everything happened in those buildings. He didn't use the mill; you could get premixed feed delivered.

"John's house was in the captain's field. He was removed from the rest of the main complex but it was still Fiddyment property; this was on the Del Webb side."

Lambing

"I recall just two barns. One had storage in the center for bailed hay. On the outside it had space for pens for sheep, holding pens. Some of the lambing would take place in the lambing barn. Some of the lambs would be born out in the field but if they could get them in then it was easier to spot them. If the mother was going into labor it was easier to monitor how the lamb was doing. Later on

when Uncle John was primarily doing the sheep it was either a vet or he was helping with the birth. He had his hand up the birth canal and grabbed the animal and pulled it out."

Memories

"Fire was a constant threat because there was so much grass lying around. If we had a wet winter there was a bumper crop of grass to burn.

"As a younger child I don't remember ever being frightened. I would roam on acres and acres of land. I knew our land. It was just open space and you and nature.

"I feel so blessed in the life I had."

The David Fiddyment Family

Top row: Deborah, Duane, Diane

Bottom row: Dolly and David

David and Dolly Giving Back

Throughout their lives David and Dolly always made giving back to their community a priority. Even in their more difficult financial situations they found a way to donate their time or money or both. Their largest and most significant donation occurred in 2006 when they were able to make a substantial gift to UC Davis.

With their focus on education, the couple made the largest private donation, $1 million, to the UC Davis School of Education, founding the Dolly and David Fiddyment Chair in Teacher Education. It is the first endowed chair for the school and one of only a handful of academic chairs nationwide focused on teacher education.

The aim is to help UC Davis inspire additional support for students interested in teaching.

To commemorate the occasion a large dinner celebration was held and daughter, Diane Fiddyment, gave the keynote. It was a monumental occasion to celebrate! The following is Diane's speech.

Diane Fiddyment Expresses Gratitude

There's no doubt about it. I was the lucky winner of the conception jackpot.

Lucky, because I'm a fifth generation Fiddyment living in California.

Lucky because my life has been touched by caring parents and great teachers.

Lucky because I come from a family that believes in giving.

When my great-great grandmother Elizabeth Jane Fiddyment came to California in 1853, she began something that is still benefiting the 7th generation of her descendants, now 165 years later. She did what every smart Californian does to this day. She bought real estate. Her foresight has provided the security and stability that has allowed every subsequent generation of this family to pursue their interests and passions.

She did something else that helped secure the future for her children and other local children. She started one of the small county school houses that came to dot the rural landscape and she became their teacher.

Elizabeth Jane was just one of the many members of my family who devoted themselves to teaching. Both of my grandmothers taught school. Cora Spangler who was to become Elizabeth's granddaughter-in-law graduated from Chico Normal School in 1910 and taught in Sacramento. My maternal grandmother, Minnetta Ritter answered the call for teachers in the new state of New Mexico around the same time. And then there is my great-aunt Gladys Ritter who began her teaching career at the age of 17. She taught in Colorado until she was 65, and then moved to Arizona where there was no mandatory retirement age. She finished 54 years of continuous teaching when she finally retired at age 71.

The most influential teachers in my life have been my parents. My brother Duane, sister Deborah, and I were lucky to live and grow up in my dad's classroom. Living on the ranch gave us continual opportunities to learn at his side. Whether it was measuring grains to be ground for turkey feed, learning to jump a ditch using a shovel as a vault, or calculating crop yields based on different cultural practices in the pistachio orchard, Dad was imparting his knowledge to us in real world situations; teaching us how to apply the vital lessons that we use throughout our lives.

Mom was a model elementary school teacher. She loved her job and reveled in the satisfaction of watching her students learn under her tutelage. I couldn't help but to absorb some of her passion, which has led me to the joy of life-long learning.

Imagine if you will, a 3rd-grader watching the papers come out for grading after the tuna casserole was cleared from the dinner table, the red pencil correcting mistakes and encouraging work well done. Imagine, one night that eight-year old helping cut out pieces of construction paper that would be used the next day to teach a lesson in fractions, and imagine that eight-year old day-by-day, acquiring the love of learning that would

eventually open the worlds of history, finance and cultural understanding that would become the passions of her life. I was that girl.

So now I want to join all of you in congratulating my parents for continuing the legacy that Elizabeth Jane and others in our family started all those years ago. It only seems natural that Mom and Dad would want to pass on to future generations of students the benefits and joys of having great teachers. But sometimes feeling natural isn't the same as the actual generosity of making a gift like this. It is very common for parents to want to see their life's accumulations pass on to their heirs, and as one of their heirs, I could be saying, "Hey, wait a minute …" But here again, Mom and Dad are teaching the valuable lessons of philanthropy and giving back. They feel that they have been so richly blessed and in turn want to provide that same security and stability that was Elizabeth's legacy, to others who follow the noble path of becoming a teacher.

Thank you Mom and Dad for being great parents and great teachers. ❧

Top: David
Bottom: Diane, Dolly

References

Fiddyment Family Letters and Diaries, 1835-1945

Interviews with David Fiddyment, Duane Fiddyment, John Fiddyment, Eric Fiddyment, by Christina Richter 2006-2012

Probate and Will documents of Elizabeth Jane Fiddyment Hill Atkinson

Roseville Public Library, oral history interview with Cora Fiddyment, March 1979

Fiddyment ranch house nomination for the National Register of Historic Places

Biographies, History of Sonoma County, 1880-90

Sonoma County History, published 1889

History of State of California Biographies, published 1906

Placer County History, published 1882

Roseville Press Tribune and Register Newspaper, various dates

Roseville Historical Society, archives

Leonard "Duke" Davis, Roseville Historian, various publications

Houghton, Eliza Donner, "The Expedition of the Donner Party"

Diane Fiddyment speech commemorating her parents' gift to UC Davis

Sacramento Bee, various articles

Placer County Archives

Ancestry.com, records database

Mountain lion shot on the Fiddyment ranch brought into town. It is lying in front of the old Sawtelle feed store, presently the Pacific Cafe.